The Fourth Book of Pilgrimages to Old Homes

Fletcher Moss

Nabu Public Domain Reprints:

You are holding a reproduction of an original work published before 1923 that is in the public domain in the United States of America, and possibly other countries. You may freely copy and distribute this work as no entity (individual or corporate) has a copyright on the body of the work. This book may contain prior copyright references, and library stamps (as most of these works were scanned from library copies). These have been scanned and retained as part of the historical artifact.

This book may have occasional imperfections such as missing or blurred pages, poor pictures, errant marks, etc. that were either part of the original artifact, or were introduced by the scanning process. We believe this work is culturally important, and despite the imperfections, have elected to bring it back into print as part of our continuing commitment to the preservation of printed works worldwide. We appreciate your understanding of the imperfections in the preservation process, and hope you enjoy this valuable book.

PILGRIMAGES
TO OLD HOMES

THE HALL OF THE HOME OF NOBLE POVERTY

THE FOURTH BOOK OF
PILGRIMAGES
TO OLD HOMES

By

FLETCHER MOSS

OF

THE OLD PARSONAGE
DIDSBURY, ESQUIRE

One of His Majesty's Justices of the Peace
for the County Palatine of Lancaster

ENGLAND

THE PHOTOGRAPHS

BY

JAMES WATTS

OF

ABNEY HALL, CHESHIRE, AND
KINDER SCOUT, DERBYSHIRE
ESQUIRE

Published by the Author from his Home
The Old Parsonage, Didsbury
1st January 1908

"GOD SAVE YOU, PILGRIM!
Whither are you bound?"
ALL'S WELL THAT ENDS WELL.

Printed by BALLANTYNE, HANSON & CO.
At the Ballantyne Press, Edinburgh

Preface

THIS book is a continuation of my other books on pilgrimages. To distinguish it from the others I name it the fourth, for when the previous one, the third, was published, buyers were often confused between the third and the second; and the confusion may increase, for peradventure others may follow, though I should be sorry to alarm any one.

Excepting some local histories, the first book I published was named "Folk-Lore, Old Customs and Tales of my Neighbours." It contained my first pilgrimages to the Royal Oak, Boscobel; Hawarden; Blore Heath; Beeston and Peckforton Castles; and Barthomley; but the contents were so very miscellaneous that, although it is similar in size and type to its followers, I omit it from the series.

No. 1 (1901) is "Pilgrimages in Cheshire and Shropshire"; and is now worth many times its original price.

No. 2 (1903) is "Pilgrimages to Old Homes mostly on the Welsh Border."

No. 3 (1906) is "Pilgrimages to Old Homes."

No. 4 (1908) is "The Fourth Book of Pilgrimages to Old Homes."

A summary of the contents of the first three is given at the end of this book.

Not one of these books has been written for pecuniary profit, and not one of them has ever been advertised. They have been written for love—love of the work; love of the pilgrimage; love of the home and its history in folk-lore and book-lore; fresh air and exercise for the body and fresh interest in life for the mind. They have worked their own way into circulation, for I have been my own publisher, and the London booksellers have rigorously boycotted them. The boycott has failed, and the London book-trade has merely lost a profit, for I find they took only thirty copies (many of them being for export) out of more than nine hundred copies that were sold and paid for of the "Welsh Border" book, 1903.

The books must increase in value as the years roll on, for the photographs show the actual buildings and their furniture—the fast disappearing houses wherein our fathers lived and died; the beds whereon they died; the chairs they sat upon; the great oak tables as worm-eaten as they are who once ate, drank, and were merry at them; the hiding-holes in which they hid in oft recurring times of trouble; in fact the homes our fathers left us, fast crumbling into dust as our fathers are.

It helps us to feel our share in the heritage of trouble or of joy from those who have gone before us if we learn some little of what has happened in these old homes. We may listen to the folk-lore and ponder over the book-lore, "many a quaint and curious volume of forgotten lore," as the grandfathers' clocks slowly tick the passing hours of the long, dark nights of winter and the ghosts of the departed hover around. "All houses wherein men have lived and died are haunted," though the stranger cannot see the ghosts the old folks living in the houses see. Old tales are told again—tales of love and hate, of jealousy and treachery, of never-ending feud, of battle, murder and sudden death, death on the scaffold or in prison, death to the innocent as well as to the guilty, and sometimes there are dim records of the happy life that has no history, some faded memorial of quiet peace and lifelong love that is all forgotten.

PREFACE

Life is too short to see a tithe of our old homes, or to hear aught of what has happened in them. I have wandered past many a time-worn hall where the owners and the contents have long since perished and all the history is utterly forgotten. The homes themselves are constantly passing away under the hurrying stress of our modern life; the exuberance of our country's wealth and restless energy is hastening the time when they will be no more. "Restoration" and decay, riches and poverty, alike are ruining them. Let the reader who cares for them tarry not; the years draw nigh when there may be no pleasure in them.

FLETCHER MOSS.

THE OLD PARSONAGE,
DIDSBURY.

Contents

	PAGE
HALL I' TH' WOOD, BOLTON LE MOORS	1
SMITHILLS HALL, THE HOUSE OF THE BLOODY FOOTMARK	19
SANDBACH	29
THE HOMES OF AUDLEY AND THE FOUR SQUIRES OF POICTIERS—AUDLEY—BETLEY—BARTHOMLEY—DODDINGTON—WRINEHILL—WYBUNBURY—MUCKLESTONE—BROUGHTON	45
THE LAND OF CASTLES—BRECON TO PEMBROKE	111
OUR SECOND PILGRIMAGE TO ST. DAVIDS	140
CONWY—PLAS MAWR—GWYDYR—DOLWYDDELAN—HARLECH—CORS Y GEDOL—CYMMER—HENGWRT—LLANEGRYN—DOLAU GWYN	176
ARUNDEL CASTLE	267
THE HOME OF NOBLE POVERTY—WINCHESTER	301
STONYHURST	322
HARDWICK HALL	346
NORMAN HALL	378
THE GUARDIANS OF THE HOME	381
HALE BARNS	385
INDEX	393

PILGRIMAGES TO
OLD HOMES

HALL I' TH' WOOD, BOLTON LE MOORS

THE first journey we made in 1906 was a veritable pilgrimage to a genuine, well-preserved old Home, where a quiet, humble man invented a machine that many-fold multiplied the manufacture of cotton goods, and thereby enormously increased the trade and wealth of England.

It seems incongruous and almost repellent to mix up cotton-spinning with these pilgrimages; but, as often stated, truth is stranger than fiction, and also more interesting. It is a fact that the hiding-hole in Hall i' th' Wood was used to hide machinery, not to hide a priest, and surely no one would doubt that the new invention did more good to the world than a multitude of priests.

It is also a strange fact that the old house is there with its old timbers in a good state of preservation, and its old name has clung to it still, though one might walk for miles and never find a wood or a moor, only the interminable streets and houses of a manufacturing town. The wood has been burnt, and the moors have been buried under acres of mills filled with machinery, all spinning like mad and making millions of money by the Hall i' th' Wood mule machine, famous wherever cotton is spun or machinery is made for the spinning of cotton yarn finer than ever was spun before poor Sam Crompton invented it here.

Hall i' th' Wood stands on a steep rock or bank, around whose base a little river flows. The site is naturally fortified, and was probably occupied by the primeval men who first came to this wild district. The timber-built part of the house, which is so picturesque, is about four hundred years old, and would originally be thatched. The stone wing is dated 1648, and bears the initials of Alexander Norris and his wife Anne. But there is an older inscribed stone over a mantelpiece with the date 1591, and the initials L. B. B.

When I first saw this fine old Hall it was in very bad repair, tumbling into ruin and utterly neglected. A farmer named Bromley lived there, but could tell very little of the history of the place. He did not think the above initials were of his family, for they had not been there much above a hundred years, and Cromptons were there "afore" them. Times were bad, of course; how could they ever be anything else for farmers in that country? It seemed heart-breaking work for everybody, but I soon heard a good tale about the place.

Two brothers of the old name of Lever were trading as grocers under the firm of Lever Brothers, Bolton, and making a large fortune out of "Sunlight" soap. One of them, who has been very generous to his native town of Bolton, was being shown over this old Hall, and he also asked about the mysterious initials, the handwriting on the wall; was there no seer who could read them? Fortunately there was a Daniel present who, with the inspiration of genius,

HAGI I' TH' WOOD

promptly interpreted them into "Lever Brothers, Bolton."

> "He read it on that night—
> The morrow proved it true."

Mr. Lever bought the place and presented it to the town of Bolton as a museum. From a guide and catalogue, with notes on its history, that are there published, we may learn the first recorded owner of Hall i' th' Wood was Lawrence Brownlow, whose will was dated 1550, and in it he, Lowrens Brounlawe, after pious bequests of his soul and body, leaves to his son Roger, who is not to sell any sapling trees, a long list of curious items with values attached in an inventory. A "gret bouster wayne with a hede yocke" may be a travelling carriage or a waggon. There are other waynes, plows, bedstocks, arkes, turnels, chystes, brasse pannes, candlesticks, &c.; six sheep are valued at sixteen shillings for the lot, hives of bees at fourpence, and thirty-five pieces of pewter at a few pence apiece. His widow, as long as she remains unmarried, may get "coles or turves . . . and have free libertie to his mylne, kylne, and sestorne."

In 1577 his grandson, Lawrence, succeeded to the estate, and doubtless his are the initials on the wall with his wife's in 1591. His first wife was named Bridget. In after years the wife's name was Elizabeth, and that shortened to Betsy or Betty may have given the B to form the L. B. B. Other owners soon came with other initials, for Christopher Norris purchased the Hall, and his son Alexander built the stone wing, putting the initials of himself and his wife with the date 1648 over the porch.

Alice, his daughter and heiress, took the property to the Starkies of Huntroyde, who put their mark on the wall, not in mere vulgar initials, but a proudly quartered coat of arms as may be seen in our picture on page 9. The John Starkie whom Alice married

HALL I' TH' WOOD

was son of Nicholas, who was blown to pieces by the treachery of the Royalists at Houghton Tower in the Civil War. The Starkies owned the Hall until 1899, when Mr. Lever bought it as before mentioned.

The fame of Hall i' th' Wood does not come from any owner, but from a poor persecuted tenant—a shy solitary man—who thought and fiddled and schemed by himself, whose invention has helped incalculably in the clothing of the people throughout the world, and has brought wealth far beyond any measure to the town, the county, and the kingdom where he was born and where his life was spent.

Sam Crompton's parents were poor farmers, spinners, and weavers, who came to the Hall when he was five years old, in 1758. His father soon died, but Betty, his mother, was a good woman, who worked long and hard to rear her three children and keep the family respectable. She was overseer of the poor for the township, but what I am better pleased to learn is that her butter fetched the top price, that her bees gathered honey for her even in that country, and that she was famed for her home-made elderberry wine. (Here, I must interject, we have two or three bottles of elderberry and damson wine that my mother made in 1834, and the last one that was opened was good.) Poor Betty Crompton! her glory must be in her son, for, with all her struggling and striving, her goods were not worth £100 when she died, and left her three children to carry on the war with the world and with poverty.

When Sam Crompton came of age he had to spin all day to earn his daily bread, to fiddle at the theatre at Bolton to earn eighteenpence a night and buy tools with the money that he might make experiments in machinery when other folk were in bed. With hard and unremitting toil for five years his success was won; by his newly invented machine he spun yarns finer

STAIRCASE AT HALL I' TH' WOOD

and better than ever were spun before; he married a wife, and prosperity blessed his early manhood. But not for long; the prosperity brought the care and the trouble that so often follow in its wake. His yarns were so good his customers would have more, the trade coveted them, the unscrupulous hungered for them and set upon him, giving him no rest, night or day. With ladders they looked in at the upper windows of the Hall to watch the conjuror of the fine spun thread, to see the wizard at his work. One adventurer hid in the roof and watched through a gimlet-hole in the ceiling. The wreckers were threatening, and the machine had hurriedly to be taken to pieces and hidden in the hiding-hole that long ago had been built in the Hall as a place of refuge for hunted men, and here was a machine worth hundreds of the men who would destroy that which was to bring them prosperity.

There are more ways of killing a dog than by hanging it, and the great men in the cotton industry got Sam Crompton's secret from him in a more respectable way than by robbery with violence. Sir Richard Arkwright called surreptitiously. Mr., afterwards Sir, Robert Peel subscribed a guinea to a fund, and called with several mechanics to see how the thing was worked, intending to copy it on their return. Neighbours and competitors agreed to buy his machine, and signed an agreement to give him the subscription opposite to their names on the paper. The highest amount to be paid was a guinea, and several who signed learned all that they wanted to learn, but paid nothing. Crompton got about £60 altogether, and the cotton-spinners who picked his brains got that which made them millions of money.

He made a new machine which he had to work himself, for if he taught apprentices they were soon tempted to leave him and set up for themselves or to

CHIMNEY BREAST WITH THE STARKIE ARMS
The hiding-hole where Crompton hid his machine is behind and above it.

teach others. He also invented an improved machine for carding or combing the cotton; and his "friends" or competitors wished to buy it, but he was so sore with the ill-usage he had already received that, with his axe, he chopped to pieces the product of his long thoughts and hard work, saying: "They shall not have this also."

Thirty years after the mule machine had been given to the public and great fortunes had been made by it, while its inventor remained poor, the beneficiaries became compassionate and said something ought to be done for Crompton. Then the cute cotton-spinners took counsel together and asked the Parliament to do it, for the country had largely profited by the invention and the subscription among themselves had only realised £60. The Members for the county were interviewed, one of the most powerful being Sir Robert Peel, the very man who had paid a guinea and gone with mechanics to copy the machine for his own enormous gain. It would only be human nature for Crompton and Peel to detest one another, and not to work well together. Mr. Perceval was the Chancellor of the Exchequer, and he was to have proposed that a reward be made, but on that same night he was shot in the lobby of the House by an assassin.

After months of delay Lord Stanley proposed and carried that £5000 be voted to Mr. Crompton for his invention. Out of this sum a considerable amount was stopped for fees and expenses, and one member tried to borrow £1000 for his share. Another had said, "Give the man £100 a year; it will be as much as he can drink." They were remarkably like town councillors of the present day, but Crompton merely wrote: "Me they cannot dishonour. All the risk is with them. The greatest honour . . . is to do me and themselves justice. I am not abegging or demanding. . . . Nine-tenths of the House wear cloth at a reduced price of forty to fifty per cent. that is spun on these machines and of a beauty which the world cannot equal. . . . When I gave up the machine to the country it was worth Fifty Thousand Pounds."

He also proved that the import duty on the cotton wool for his machines had risen to £300,000 a year, therefore his valuation might have been multiplied many fold. Let us also refute that calumny about the "drink," for the slanderers, like the poor, are always with us. The brain that conceived the great invention was nurtured on oatmeal and milk, not on the "drink" of the mischief-maker.

With the balance of the money received Crompton went into the cotton business again, but he was too shy and sensitive to have any chance in business. The money gradually slipped away, and he spent much time in inventing new mechanism for weaving patterns in fancy muslins, but when he produced anything good some one quickly copied it in inferior quality, undersold him, and brought down more depression in the days of declining strength and grey hairs.

Although my knowledge of machinery is very slight, the reading of the various little histories of Sam Crompton made me wishful to know more of the great invention that is in use to-day and has so miraculously increased the cotton manufactures of the world. After having asked several men who are owners of enormous mills, and others engaged very largely in the trade, I found they knew next to nothing and cared less about Sam Crompton and his almost forgotten invention, but at the School of Technology, Manchester, where they teach you anything and everything, I was shown the process of cotton-spinning with all the best and latest appliances, and young men from the uttermost ends of the earth learning it, and there the mule and spindle carriage of Crompton were explained.

Much less than two hundred years ago all the cotton that ever was spun in any land was spun by hand in single threads. About 1767 a poor, illiterate, hand-loom weaver named Hargreaves, here, in our county of Lancaster, invented a machine whereby he could spin eight threads on eight separate spindles all at the same time, and the number of spindles was soon multiplied. Then his grateful countrymen formed themselves into gangs and smashed all the multiplying machines, while he had to flee for his life. About the same time Arkwright adopted the plans of others for spinning cotton, by passing it through pairs of rollers revolving at different speeds. Crompton learned to spin on a jenny of Hargreaves, to which he added rollers and an improved carriage for his spindles, making the machine celebrated as the mule.

The cotton yarn or thread is passed through two or three pairs of revolving rollers that elongate it, on to revolving spindles that rapidly twist it and recede from the rollers faster than the yarn is delivered to them. When the spindles are at the end of their tether the rollers stop, a slight rod, called the faller, drops on to the row of threads, pushing them to the lower part of the spindles round which they wind as the spindles retreat back to the rollers and all begin again, the fine threads being thereby spun or drawn out and twisted finer than by any other method.

By this fine spinning Crompton doubled the length of thread he could get from a pound of cotton and trebled its value. For, he said, on his old machine he could only spin No. 40, that is yarn of forty hanks (of 840 yards) to the pound of cotton, for which he was paid fourteen shillings; but with his new machine he could spin No. 60, or sixty hanks, and get twenty-five shillings; and he did make some No. 80, and receive two guineas for it. On the day of my writing this I am told the prices of these counts of

THE WITHDRAWING-ROOM, HALL I' TH' WOOD

yarn in Manchester are: for forties, elevenpence; for sixties, seventeen pence; for eighties, nineteen pence. What an enormous drop! From forty-two shillings to nineteen pence, though every one concerned is far better off than they were then. Cotton-spinners, like butchers, "live by their losses." All trades have been bad ever since I knew them, that is, if we believe the folk who are in them, but this cotton trade seems to surpass all, for, in addition to the great reduction in price, there has been the enormous increase in the imports. When Crompton brought out his mule machine the imports of raw cotton into Great Britain from all countries were from four to six millions of pounds a year. In a few years they grew to thirty-two millions, and for 1906 they are estimated to have been twenty-one thousand million pounds in the year.

Let us also note that in our time, even to-day, there is more fine spinning of cotton round Hall i' th' Wood than there is round any other centre in the world.

The Hall itself is now a museum, containing many relics of Crompton and a stone press for the making of cheese that was in it long before his day, and has never been removed, for it is mentioned in the inventory of the goods of Alexander Norris, 1672, as being valued at "£000, 03, 00." There are cotton plants and many wonderful fabrics made from cotton. The organ and the fiddle made by Crompton are carefully preserved with his bible, his music, chair, axe, knife, &c. But several high-backed, rush-seated chairs that once were his found a home elsewhere, for X has treasured them at Abney Hall for many years. After Crompton's death they were sold to the tenant of the Starkie Arms Inn, Tong Moor, and when that house was rebuilt they were sold by auction.

The rooms are furnished with genuine good furniture of about the same age as the house. The withdrawing-room, as shown on page 13, has been re-

OLD FURNITURE

panelled with oaken panelling from another old manor-house, and has an ornamental plaster ceiling reproduced from another in Bolton. The oak settle with box-seat, the child's chair, the curfew in the fireplace, and the

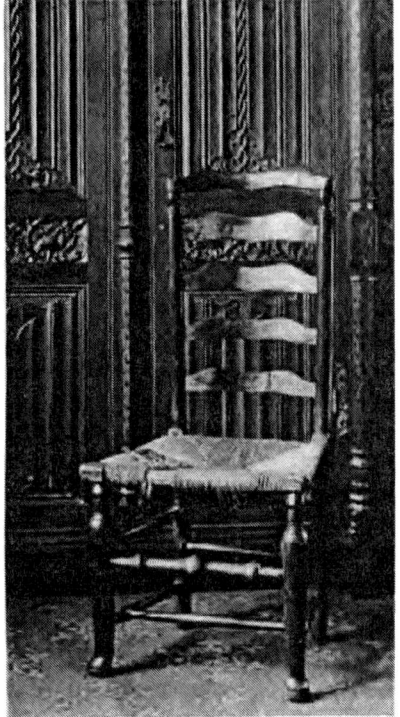

ONE OF SAM CROMPTON'S CHAIRS

fine tapestried chair are all shown in the picture. There is a rare livery cupboard, a piece of furniture that is almost unknown in our time; it was the receptacle for hot or newly-baked bread, the dole of charity bread dealt out in churches, or the supper reserved for late or early guests in houses,

There are old pictures, pewter, pottery, puzzle jugs, and curiosities. The whole place is beautifully kept, and is in such good taste that I wondered greatly who controlled it. All that I could learn was that the borough of Bolton owned it, and that Mr. Lever found any money that might be wanted; but who finds the brains?

If we could only have a place like this in Manchester! There is one of about the same age, with a moat round it, that is owned by the city, and known as Clayton Hall, the home of Manchester's most famous citizen, Humphrey Chetham. But our city council have sadly mauled it. One of their number was what is termed a "decorator," and he was entrusted to "decorate" it. So he "decorated" it according to the "decorations" 'mid which he had been reared—cheap cottage paper on old hall walls, churchwarden's whitewash or dauby paint on russet oak that time had mellowed—and then he died.

It is a sad tale is this of poor Sam Crompton and the old Hall i' th' Wood that, throughout all time to come and wheresoever in the world the cotton fibre is manufactured into clothing, will be for ever famous by his genius. See him struggling to piece the broken threads, and to prevent them from breaking while he draws and twists them finer. His little son, just learning to walk, is in the dolly tub, trampling the cotton in the soapsuds till the dollop is ready for the carding and the spinning. Their food is oatmeal, their amusement is music. Well he knows

"The spurns that patient merit of the unworthy takes."

Neighbours and strangers alike are ever on the watch, prying into his business, to learn how he makes the fine yarns they cannot make. If he buys a nail at the blacksmith's, the curiosity of many is roused as to whether it really was a nail, what the size of it might be, and how he was going to use it. One little tale that is told of him may cause a smile, but it shows the calm thought of the man. A lady told him Bonaparte had married the Archduchess of Austria, and she hoped they might have a family. Crompton's quiet reply was, "Do you want a breed on 'em."

A man of his temperament naturally abhorred war, longed for peace, retrenchment, and reform, and

LIVERY CUPBOARD AT HALL I' TH' WOOD

gradually he slipt from the Church and became a Swedenborgian. The unsuspecting innocence of his younger days was bitterly wronged, and his sensitive nature was soured by the unscrupulousness of the men with the muck-rake, whose riches grew from his invention while he was left to pine in poverty and solitude.

In after years the heirs of those who starved him gave in the prodigality of their wealth their spare coppers to set up on high in their busy streets an image of the man their fathers robbed.

18   PILGRIMAGES TO OLD HOMES

If this statue of Crompton should fire some budding genius to emulate his example and to do some good to his fellow-men, let him reflect—though his neighbours may deify him when he is dead, some of them will, if they can, wrong him to the uttermost farthing, and leave him to starve and die in poverty.

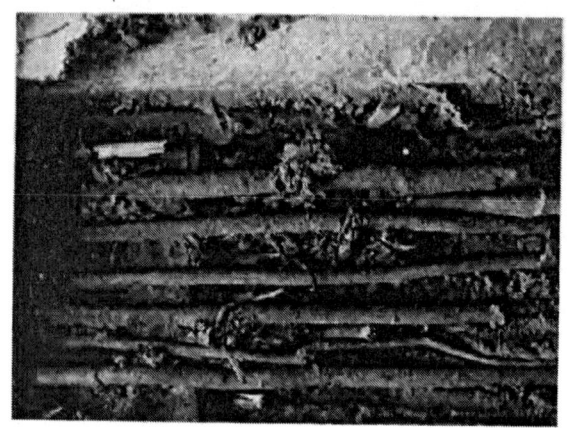

OAKEN BEAM AND WATTLE WORK IN HALL I' TH' WOOD

SMITHILLS HALL—THE HOUSE OF THE BLOODY FOOTMARK

MY last book recorded a pilgrimage to the House of the Skull, the pilgrimage here recorded is to the House of the Bloody Footmark. The skull is that of a martyr for his faith. The footmark is that of a martyr for his faith. But the martyrdoms were for different faiths or creeds, and, in each case, the victim was of the same faith as the murderers in the other. The old Halls are within seven miles of one another and of Hall i' th' Wood, where Crompton suffered starvation for inventing that which enriched millions. Father Ambrose or Barlow, whose skull we photographed at the fine old moated Hall of Wardley, was hanged, drawn, and quartered because he was a Roman Catholic priest, no charge of crime being brought against him. George Marsh, who stamped his foot at Smithills, was burnt at Chester because he would not be a Roman Catholic. Both sides of professing Christians burnt or cut up the bodies for the good of the souls of those who differed from them. Verily the ways of our forefathers were wonderful, and it is well for us to know more about them that we may try to do better.

I prefer to read history from contemporary records if any can be found, and the lives and deaths of the martyrs written by Foxe and printed in 1583 has a long account of Marsh, with a picture of him chained to the stake with the fire blazing around him and molten pitch dropping on him—a fierce looking man with a big poleaxe or javelin standing by.

Marsh was a young man living at Deane near to Smithills. He was a farmer, who had taken Orders as a curate, and would not conform to the reversion to Roman Catholicism under Queen Mary. When busy with plowing and seeding he had a summons to the local Justice of the Peace, Sir Roger Barton of Smithills Hall. Here are extracts from his own account :—

"So betimes in the morning I arose and after I had said the English Letany (as my custome was) with other praiers kneeling on my knees I prepared myselfe to go towards Smethehills and I was going thitherward . . . to comfort my mother and be good to my litle children for they shoulde not see my face any more until the last daie and so tooke my leave of them not without teares shed on both parties and soe I came to Smethehilles about nine of the clock and presented myselfe afore magster Barton who shewed me a letter fro the earle of Darby wherein he was commanded to send mee with others to Lathum."

There and then, it would be, that Marsh stamped his foot to shake off the dust of the house of him who sent the poor curate on his hopeless course towards the dreadful fire; and the bloody footmark on the threshold of the fine old Hall is there to this day.

At Lathom Marsh was examined on Palm Sunday by Sir John Biron, the vicar of Prescot, Sir William Nores, Sir Pierce a Lee (Legh) and a Maister Schereburn. He was ordered to give answers in writing to four questions about the Mass, transubstantiation, and confession, and was sent to Lancaster Castle. He said "questions engender strife," and, though many priests argued with him, "priests be not alwaies the greatest clerks."

Dr. Cotes, the Bishop of Chester, or Westchester, as it was then called, had him brought to him that he might have the pleasure of reviling the heretic personally, for he said, "Non disputandum est cum haeretico," and when he lapsed into the vulgar tongue the episcopal language was shocking.

THE TERRACE, SMITHILLS HALL

In the Chapel of Our Lady in Chester Cathedral before the Mayor, Fulk Dutton, Dr. Wall, and others, Marsh actually said that the Bishop of Rome ought not to exercise authority in England, so the Bishop of Chester called him "a most damnable, irreclaimable, and unpardonable heretic," and the Chancellor called him a "scabbed sheep of the flock." The Bishop then took up a paper and put his spectacles upon his nose to

read the condemnation; whereupon the Chancellor, with a glavering and smiling countenance, asked my Lord to stay a while and pray. The Bishop read to the end and said, "Now wyll I no more pray for thee than I wyll for a dogge." Marsh answered he would pray for him.

From the Cathedral he was delivered to the "Shiriffes of the Citie," who, with men armed with poleaxes, thrust him into a dark dungeon at the Northgate, from whence, on the 24th of April 1555, he was led with fettered feet to be burnt alive outside the city walls at Spittle-boughton.

Vawdrey, "the deputie chamberleine," offered him a pardon if he would recant, if he would "come into the catholicke church." Many people offered him money to buy Trentals of Masses for his soul, and this offering of money to a man who is about to be killed is one of the most incomprehensible parts of the proceedings.

Marsh stedfastly went his way to the torture, refused all their offers, and asked them not to burn his old clothes for they might be useful to some poor sinner.

"And so kneeling downe he made his praiers and then put off his clothes unto his shirte then was he chained unto the post having a number of Faggottes under him and a thing made like a firkin with pitch and tarre in the same ouer his head and by reason the fire was unskilfullye made and that the winde did dribe the flame to and froe he suffered great extremitie in his deathe, whiche notwithstanding, he abode very pacientlie.

"Wherein this in him is to be noted, that when he had bin a long time tormented in the fire without mooving having his fleshe so broiled and pufte up that they which stoode before him unneth could see the chaine wherewith hee was fastened and therefore supposed no lesse but he had bin dead, notwithstanding sodainly hee spred abroad his armes saying Father of heauen haue mercie upon me and so gielded his spirite unto the handes of the Lorde.

"Upon this many of the people saide that hee was a martyr and died marvelous patiently and godlye which caused the Bishoppe to make a sermon in the cathedral and affirm that Marsh was a hereticke burnt like an hereticke and was a firebrand in Hell."

As one small token of the truth of this dark tragedy there is the bloody footmark still at Smithills. Of course it is not bloody, nor is it of the shape or size of human foot. How could it be? after three hundred and fifty-two years of wear and tear, of rubbings and scrubbings. It is a depression of a reddish hue, and rather larger than a man's footmark on the grey stone flags by the door. Unbroken and continuous tradition has always said that is where the martyr stood when he was first brought into the presence of "Justice." He asked for justice but they gave him Law.

Smithills, or Smethells (possibly Smooth-hills originally) has a fine fourteenth-century hall of enormous oaken timbers, open roof, and vesica-shaped quatrefoils at the ends. There are also other rooms of great age, with ornamental ceilings and oaken panelling. With a chapel they form three sides of a quadrangle, and modern additions make a long house of many gables projecting on to a terrace from which a park slopes steeply down to a brook, and beyond are the chimneys and the smoke of Lancashire.

The original rent of the manor of Smithills is said to have been a pair of gilt spurs and free use of the cellars for one week per annum; but as there was no stipulation as to what was to be in the cellars, and gilt spurs are not much worn nowadays, the old-fashioned rent or feudal tenure has lapsed.

Fifty years ago Nathaniel Hawthorne slept at Smithills and never forgot "The Bloody Footstep." It would seem from his writings that he almost regretted the ghosts were kept away by the family prayers and the chapel. We looked into the chapel, but some glaring glass soon sent us out again, and the rows of cheap modern chairs in the great hall, with the Salvation Army texts on its broad beams above, to us looked very incongruous. The bloody footmark is preserved; why not preserve the rooms around it as they were in the days of Sir Roger and the martyr?

It is commonly supposed that people may now be of any religion they choose, but sometimes difficulties arise. I was lately one of a committee of Justices visiting a prison, and a prisoner was brought up who wished to change his religion. He had been entered as a Roman Catholic, but he wanted to be "Church." He could give no reason for the change beyond saying he had been wrong and now wanted to be right. The governor of the gaol told him he had done five years in another prison where his entry was marked R. C. He

SMITHILLS HALL

meekly replied that was so, but now he was converted, though we could not find out who had converted him. He was sent back, and the governor explained that the truth of the case probably was some old pal of his was now in the prison and had said his religion was Church of England; if the two could get together at prayers or service, they might enjoy one another's conversation. Hence the conversion.

After that little digression, I should like to add that this our pilgrimage to Hall i' th' Wood and Smithills was the only pilgrimage we ever made in a hansom cab. Bolton's streets are steep and slippery, paved with granite and scored with tram-lines, stretching out through miles of grimy shops or houses. There could not be pleasure, and there would certainly be danger, if we tried to cycle, so we went there by rail and hired a hansom to the Halls. The skin-and-bones we sat behind scrattled up the hills and safely sluthered down; we sat tight and nothing happened, but, when the day's work was done, the Jehu looked as if he expected a quarrel about his fare and longed for it. Nothing had been said as to miles or hours. He asked plenty and got it with more beside, for X gave him a piece of gold, telling him to keep it. The cabman's fiery face turned Tyrian purple and various shades of colour by unbidden blushes as he lost his wrangle with thoughts too many for words. He never spoke, but touched his hat, and I ventured to suggest he might give old skin-and-bones a good supper and a rest.

On my return home I was struck by the great difference there was in the leaves and flowers at Smithills and at Didsbury. The former place is only sixteen miles north-west of the latter, but there seemed to be a month's difference in the progress of the spring. I did not see a flower, and scarcely a leaf or green grass at Smithills, while my own garden was crowded with wallflowers, daffodils, polyanthus, and arabis, with plum-

THE OLDEST PART OF SMITHILLS HALL

trees in bloom and pear-trees blossoming. It seemed to be winter at one place while spring was at the other. The one was smoky, dull, and grey, the other green, and bright, and lively with the songs of birds who carolled

"to and fro
As free and blithe as if on earth
Were no such thing as woe."

A BIT OF SMITHILLS HALL

SANDBACH

IT seems late in life for me to be writing of a pilgrimage to Sandbach, when every year—and often several times in the year—I have journeyed through or near to the little town on my way to my relatives in Staffordshire. The celebrated crosses of Sandbach were the goal of many a genuine pilgrimage for centuries, and though they have been broken into bits and the bits have been carted away for miles, built into buildings, burned, and used for paving stones, they have been coming together again bit to bit after all their ill-treatment and wanderings, and the battered crosses stand again in the market-place above the din and the squalor of the market, and here are pictures of what remains of them after twelve hundred years of wear and tear.

It is said they were erected to commemorate the first preaching of Christianity in the kingdom of Mercia, and they were probably thrown down at the time of the great Civil War. Sir John Crewe of Utkinton set up the main part of the larger cross on his estate, carefully covering the crucified Christ with mortar, as he considered it to be a badge of popery, and his dread of popery was greater than his reverence for his Christ. From there this fragment went to Tarporley Rectory, and from thence to Oulton Hall. The lower part of the great cross had been built into the town well in Sandbach, and the end of the pillar was in a garden rockery. The top of the smaller cross was used as a step to a house, and other parts were

THE CROSSES, SANDBACH (THE EASTERN FACE)

THE CROSSES, SANDBACH

made into pavement. The bits were pieced with other bits, and a brass records "the liberality" of a man, who stole the greater part, in restoring the fragments.

The crosses stand on the old platform, and the old figures at the angles of the steps are still there, though they are worn away to almost shapeless stumps by the dirty children who seem to be always idly rubbing against them. The present height of the greater cross is given as sixteen feet eight inches, and of the lesser twelve feet. They have had circular heads, and the height of the larger from the ground has been estimated to have been originally from twenty-four to twenty-five feet. It undoubtedly commemorates scenes in the life of Christ, while the smaller cross is thought to record the first local preachers of Christianity.

Our photograph of the east side shows three figures in a circle, the outer ones apparently doing obeisance to the middle one. Above that are three figures, the one to the right having a dove above, the one to the left being probably Peter with the Keys. Higher again is a very plain representation of the Nativity, with the animals looking at the manger, and above that the crucified Christ with the four evangelists and their emblems at the four corners. Still higher is a figure with head downwards and others indistinct and mutilated.

The northern side shows eleven apostles being breathed on by a flying monster having a terrible triple cloven tongue.

The heads of the crosses are thought to have been circular, pierced with figures as spokes in a wheel.

The church has been so thoroughly restored by Sir Gilbert Scott, I had better say nothing about it; the spire has gone altogether. The old registers remain, and one entry seems to me to be worth copying. It is as follows:—

"1598. Baptized Williams Leversage son of William

THE BEAR INN

Leversage gentleman was baptized the fifth day of June: William Leversage, William Bulkeley, Esquires, William Yardley, William Lawton, William Moreton, William Smethwicke, William Allen, William Hassall, William Llandyn and Elizabeth Delves being the godparents and sponsors of the said child."

There would doubtless be a great "do" and jollification, to use the vulgar tongue of Cheshire, and much ale would be drunk, for I find the following praise of the Sandbach ale was elsewhere recorded about the time of this Christening:—

"Our Ale is famous for a true nappe, and I have heard men of a deep experience in that element contend for the worth of it, for true dagger stuffe. If Ale got name from Oel, the old Danish word . . . this is almost as substantiall as Oyl. . . ."

I might demur and say, if the ale is like oil how can it be nappy or brisk with a good head of foam. In either case it might be "dagger stuff," or that which would enable the "boozer" to get "forrader."

There are many ale-houses in the little town, where any one who has a penny may sample the "dagger stuff," and some of these old inns are very picturesque, for licensed houses last much longer than ordinary houses, though their tenants have much shorter lives than similar folk in other occupations.

The Bear is dated 1634 with the initials R. K. The old Hall is dated 1656 with the initials T. B. I cannot find any history of this old house or its original owners. It is doubtless on the site of the first fortress or manor-house, for it is near to the church, and on a steep bank above a brook that appears to have nearly surrounded it. It occurred to me the parish registers might show who T. B. was, and he was probably the schoolmaster Thomas Baily, who died in the year of the building of the Hall. Folk-lore tells us that men who build grand houses generally die as soon as the house is finished; and the schoolmasters of Sandbach had very unusual help from lands devoted to education.

THE OLD HALL INN

At the top of the stairs in the old Hall there remains a good specimen of a dog-gate, with primitive paling across the landing so that dogs lame or sharp, two-legged or four-legged, might be debarred from getting into the bedrooms.

THE OLD HALL INN

THE DOG-GATE AT THE OLD HALL

The old home that we went forth to see is named Abbeyfield; formerly it was the Abbot's Field, or Field House, the land having been owned in pre-reformation times by the Abbot of Dieulacres. Some stones on a small island overgrown with trees and bushes may mark the site of the first dwelling. The present house is shown in our photograph beyond the old moat.

ABBEYFIELD

There is one room in it that must be duly recorded, for I should think it is unique in our virtuous days. It is the cockpit over the dining-room. The latter is a fine room, but had been rather low. The ceiling was raised about a yard, and consequently the rooms above were spoilt, as they were then only five feet or thereabouts in height, and the late Mr. Woolf was six feet six inches, and had sons taller than himself. A large room in a country house where men could not stand upright, but could sit down secure from

ABBEYFIELD

intrusion, was evidently well adapted to be a cockpit; and there were good-looking game-birds to be seen on the premises, some of them having travelled from Didsbury.

For twenty-five years a branch of the Woolf family had lived here; the old couple were dead and the next generation (shown on page 43 of my last book) would not stay in the house. There had been six deaths there in their time, and others shortly before. The bit of old folk-lore about the ill-luck attending the confiscated lands of the religious houses turned up again. It may be another of my relatives lived there much further back, for I came across the following bit in a Chester paper of long ago, and though my father, John Moss, had an uncle John Moss, I cannot trace this John, who apparently left no children.

"On Monday the 21st of January 1771 (at his own Hall formerly called Field House, near Sandbach) died John Moss, gentleman, aged 82 years, and perfectly sensible to the last. He was an Honest Man, a sincere Friend, a kind Master, and a loving and peaceable Neighbour."

Epitaphs are said to lie like lawyers; but as there is nothing to show this eulogium was untrue, let us believe it was another instance where the hoary head is a crown of glory.

About three miles to the south or south-west of Didsbury is a big, lonely, well-built house that is seldom inhabited, and is known as Moss's folly. The only bit of history I could ever learn about it is, that it was built by two brothers named Moss, who were parsons from Sandbach; but, as there never were parsons of that name at Sandbach, the true tale is a mystery still.

About the time of the Civil War it was written "the scituation of this Town (Sandbitch) is very delightsome" but the times were not delightsome. There was a family named Steele of Giddy Hall, one of whose members was

Captain in charge of Beeston Castle, when he surrendered it to the Royalists. For this he was tried in Nantwich Church and condemned to be shot. A grave was dug, and two soldiers shot him there and then. One shot him in the belly and one in the throat. They tumbled his warm body into the grave and hilled him up.

About a month before, in the neighbouring parish of Barthomley, a far worse tragedy than this had been done. It was on Christmas Eve (1643) the anniversary of the angels' song of "peace on earth, good will to men," a troop of Royalists came to Barthomley when unarmed Roundheads were in the church. Christmas was not Merry Christmas then, for the soldiers of "God and the King" cut the throats of twelve of the Puritans, stripped their bodies, and left them. Two of them were named Steele, and were probably from Sandbach. The names of others are in my book on Folk-Lore. The church registers of the date are mutilated, for the parson told me the massacre was done by "the wrong side."

Some of the last embers of the Civil War flickered out here, when Lesley's horse, fleeing from Worcester towards Scotland, were, from utter weariness, compelled to rest for the night at Sandbach. It was on a market-day, Thursday the 4th of September, in the afternoon when the day's work would be mostly done and the bargains of the Cheshire farmers duly cemented or washed down with ale, that the foremost of the Scots who had been hurrying northwards for a night and a day after the battle with doubtless many goings astray, arrived at the little town in quest of food and rest. They were worn out and helpless, so the countrymen soon got plucky and made hay while they could, whether they were King's men or crop-ears. The Cheshire farmers would not mind a horse being tired if it was cheap enough. Two of them with a dog surrounded sixteen Scots and took them prisoners. Some were killed and buried quickly, for the townsmen shot at

THE CHURCH OF THE MASSACRE

THE CHURCH OF THE MASSACRE

them from windows. Many sheltered and were kept as prisoners in the church. The foremost escaped, though their numbers kept dwindling, as stragglers could not go on without food or rest, and the last of them surrendered at the well-known place that was then called Diddesbury.

BLISS

THE HOMES OF AUDLEY AND THE FOUR SQUIRES OF POICTIERS

ON Monday the nineteenth of September, 1356, amid the vineyards of sunny France, there was fought the great battle of Poictiers; and very strange it is to tell that some of the consequences of that battle may be seen in Cheshire to-day; for in the park at Doddington, in the midst of a great estate that was bought by the spoils of the plundered French, and that has been held for five hundred and fifty years by the descendants of the Cheshire squire who fought through the battle, the time-worn effigies of Sir James Audley and his four squires still keep their watch and ward over the land whose heirs have always honoured them.

In the early part of that long struggle, known as the hundred years of war (though it would be hard to find when there was a hundred years of peace) between France and England, the Black Prince led his army up the Garonne, pillaging and plundering all that rich land until their horses scarce could move under the spoil. Seeking fresh fields to conquer and emboldened with success, he turned towards Paris, when suddenly he was confronted with the French King at the head of an exceeding great army. Every noble, knight, and squire in France had been summoned to avenge the insult to their country, and the Black Prince was haughtily told to surrender himself with a hundred of his knights as prisoners of war. There were sixty thousand French-

TWO OF THE FOUR SQUIRES

TWO OF THE FOUR SQUIRES

men against eight thousand English; but the English were not a breed that readily surrenders—they were adventurers rather fond of a fight, and there are many chances in war.

When I was at school we were brought up in the belief that any good English lad could "lick" three Frenchmen, because we were fed on beefsteaks and ale (bull-beef sometimes), while the poor Mounseers had to live on frogs and snails with sour wine, the wonder being how "they had the cheek to stick up to us."

We must have inherited our bumptiousness with other qualities from our forefathers who fought at Poictiers, for they did valiantly against tremendous odds, and fortunately the chronicles of Froissart have preserved many interesting details of the battle.

The English army was drawn up on rising ground among the vineyards by Sir James Audley, and he begged of the Prince to be allowed to take the post of honour and danger, as he had vowed he would not spare himself throughout the coming fight. "The Prince sayde, Sir James, god gyue you this day that grace to be the best Knight of all." The quotation is from the translation of Froissart by Lord Berners, who made it by order of King Henry VIII.; that probably accounting for the little g in God, while kings and knights are spelt with capital letters.

The only road up the hill among the vineyards was so narrow between its hedges that four men could hardly ride abreast. Near the end, and in its narrowest part, Sir James Audley placed himself with his four squires, to bear the brunt of the attack, but he lined the hedges and sheltering vines or thorns with archers—the famous archers of Cheshire and the Welsh borderland, whose constant warfare for generations with their neighbours had perfected in their hands the finest weapon the world had produced. All the great victories of the English from Crecy to Flodden, or for two

IN DODDINGTON PARK

hundred years, were won by the bowmen of the Welsh border. Their long bows of yew were far more powerful than any bows known to the French or Normans. And all along the beautiful country from Chester to Cardiff or Chepstow there are yew trees standing now with long sheltering arms in the quiet churchyards, whose boughs made the bows (bous) that won us many a hard-fought fight.

About four thousand—that is, half of the little force of the English were archers. The French were confident of success by their overpowering numbers and the weight of their heavy cavalry. Three thousand of them were knights clad in complete armour impervious to lance or sword, but woefully heavy and unwieldy. They put their trust in horses that should trample under foot these English dogs, and great was their eagerness to be foremost in the attack.

Up the narrow lane and the vineyards, where the blood of the ripe grapes soon mingled with the blood of men, came the heavy armoured knights of the impetuous French, and, whistling through the air, fled long arrows from unseen foes far away—arrows that pierced the strongest armour of plate or mail as if it were eggshell, arrows that pinned the armour on to the man inside it, that sometimes pinned the rider to his horse, and oftenest and best of all maddened the stricken horse till he threw his clumsy rider. None that fell could mount again. The crush was too great, the confusion was terrible, for more cavalry were constantly coming on, shot and stung with arrows from afar. They trampled on themselves instead of on their foes, while their riderless horses galloped back by instinct and spread confusion in the camp. "They flang and toke on so feersley they fell on their own maisters." More of the French were trodden and crushed by their comrades than were slain by the sword of the English. The weight and the numbers

of the knights and their horses proved their ruin; they knew not "which way to turn" as the goose-winged shafts of Cheshire struck like goads through the armour they deemed impenetrable — the splendid armour that was worse than useless when the lightning struck them.

The confusion of the French became so great that the King himself with his son and staff with seventeen earls were taken prisoners. The English men-at-arms ran in, slew who they caught, and "dyd what they lyst." But the English are a practical race, sometimes fond of a fight, but oftener fonder of money, and they soon found it would pay better to take a Frenchman prisoner and get a ransom than it would to stick him. Therefore they took prisoners; every Englishman having about two Frenchmen whom he had surrounded, and claimed as his private property. They tied them together, or to carts, or to anything while terms of ransom could be arranged. The terms were fairly easy, for prisoners were plentiful and cheap, but if the captured ones had nothing, and could get or promise nothing—well—they might as well be dead.

All through the long day of battle and tumult, stout Sir James Audley and his four squires held the pass of the narrow lane, and no Frenchmen got beyond them to the camp of the Prince. I use the word stout as it is used in his country to-day. It means strong and determined, of a good courage—not a fat beast. "He was soore hurte in the bodye and in the vysage, but as longe as his breth serued hym he foughte, then they layd hym under a hedgesyde to sew up his wounds."

After the battle the Prince asked for him, and eight of his men carried him in a litter to the Black Prince, who thanked him, "kyst hym, and made hym great chere," deeming him the best knight in the battle, and settling on him five hundred marcs a year secured on estates in England.

STAIRWAY, DODDINGTON CASTLE

Then he was carried from the royal presence to his own tent, where he summoned all his relatives who were in the battle, as if he expected death, and to them he said: "My lords and gentlemen, you see these four squires, what glory I have gained has been through their 'valyantnesse.' I give to them . . . the gift of my lord the prince. I disinherit myself of it and give it to them simply without possibility of revoking it."

Then the lords and knights looked on each other and said: "May the Lord remember you for it! We will bear witness of this gift to them wheresoever and whensoever we be come."

The Prince soon heard of this devolution of his reward, and sent for Sir James to ask him if the grant to him had not been agreeable to him, or if it had not sufficed him.

"Yes, my Lord," was the reply; "it was most agreeable to me. These four squyers have served me long and loyally in many dangerous besynesses. At this last batayle they served me in such wyse that had they never done nothynge els I was bounde to reward them, and they had never nothinge of me in rewarde before. Sire, I am but a man alone; but by the ayde and comfort of them I had been deed in the batayle, and they had not ben; wherefore, sir, I had not ben curtesse if I wolde not a rewarded them. I thanke God, my Lord, I have had and shall have ynough as long as I lyve, I will never be abasshed for lacke of good. Pardon me, sir: both I and my squyers shall serve you as well as ever we dyd."

Then the Black Prince confirmed the gift to them; and in addition settled six hundred marcs a year on Sir James Audley.

The spoil of the French camp, the richest armour, the gold and the silver plate and the ornaments, the jewels, the furs, the tents, and the harness, all fell into the hands of the English with the coin or goods

DODDINGTON CASTLE

that were demanded for the ransoms of half the nobility of France. Most of the English had not tasted bread for three days, but at last they could make up for arrears, and out of his own provisions and at his own table the captured King was treated royally.

The Prince took care to retreat as quickly as he could to a seaport, so as to get his prisoners and plunder to England as soon as possible; but they had to tarry long at Bordeaux, where many of the English, in true English fashion, wasted their new riches in riot and revelry.

When the English ships were ready there was trouble with the Gascons, who demurred to the King of France being taken out of the country. But all a Gascon loves or desires is money. (So Froissart says; let us hope the poor Gascon is no worse than others.) The Prince paid them a hundred thousand florins to soothe their ruffled breasts, and then he embarked with the King his prisoner. They were eleven days and nights at sea—what a lively passage! They safely arrived at Sandwich; on the third day came to Canterbury; on the morrow to Rochester; then to Dartford, next to London.

In the triumphal march through London the King of France rode on a white charger richly caparisoned, while the Black Prince rode on a little black hackney by his side. They went to the palace of the Savoy and afterwards to Windsor. Here let us take leave of them and get back to Cheshire whence our four squires came and where they doubtless took their booty home.

Sir James Audley, K.G., the hero of Poictiers, was an illegitimate son of another Sir James Audley, or Audeley, or Auldithlegh, who was son to one lord and brother to another Baron of Audley, a manor and parish where Staffordshire borders on Cheshire. Sir James became one of the first Knights of the

AUDLEY TO THE LEFT. HELEY CASTLE VISIBLE IN THE DISTANCE. WRINEHILL AND DODDINGTON TO THE RIGHT. CREWE BEHIND

Garter, had large estates granted to him from the land of the plundered French, and a glorious funeral at Poictiers thirteen years after the battle. His four famous squires were Delves of Doddington, Dutton of Dutton, Fowleshurst of Crewe, and Hawkstone of Wrinehill. The squires had well won the spurs of knighthood.

About six miles to the west of Audley is Doddington, the long descended home of the heirs of Sir John Delves, whither we are wending now on pious pilgrimage.

Midway between the two is Wrinehill. I think the boundary of the counties divides the present village. The daughter of Sir John Hawkstone married an Egerton, and some of that numerous family owned the land for many years, and part of it they own to-day.

About six miles to the north-west, or north of Audley, Wrinehill, and Doddington, is Crewe, now famous as a great railway-station, but then a lonely village, part of the estate of Robert Fowleshurst, another of the four squires. His mailed effigy is still on his time-worn tomb in Barthomley, the church of the Massacre (pages 42 and 43). Crue was in the parish of Barthomley, and for eight generations was owned by the Fowleshursts; the fifth of them, another Robert, left his bones where so many of the men of Cheshire "returned not again," on the bleak hills of Flodden.

Any one with a knowledge of the country, or even with an ordnance map, may see that Audley, Wrinehill, Doddington, and Crewe, or their respective parishes, join one another. There remains Robert Dutton of Dutton to be accounted for. Dutton Hall is many miles to the north-west, but there were several branches of the family scattered about Cheshire and its neighbourhood. It has been noted the Audleys owned part of Maer a little further to the south; and Duttons owned the other part. In the adjoining parish of Standon there were two Robert Duttons about this time. They were relations of Robert de Standon, the lord of the manor who bore the Dutton Arms;

THE TOMB OF SIR ROBERT FOWLESHURST

therefore my old Standon coffer may have been their strong box.

As an instance of the tenacity of names of men and places, I notice the name of the man who commonly waits on me at table now is Robert Dutton, and our farming man for many years was "owd Jimmy Authley."

BETLEY

BETLEY OLD HALL

John Delves, Esquire, while engaged in the war in France bought Dodyington or Dodinton in 1352. It would then be forest land in the parish of Wybunbury, and on it he had license to build a castle or fortified house in 1364. Poictiers had then been won, and

BETLEY OLD HALL

the young squire may have been at the previous battle of Crecy and the taking of Calais. He invested his plunder of the French in land in Cheshire and the neighbouring counties, thereby showing he was a better man of business than his superior officer who accepted great estates in the conquered country. It was only a matter of time for them to be lost again, but Sir James Audley had his time in them, and left his dust to mingle with the dust he had won.

AUDLEY HALL

Sir John Delves was buried at Audley, and as we learnt his effigy was still in the church, another day's pilgrimage was made to it. We took Barthomley on the way to pay our respects to Sir Robert Fowleshurst, but he was locked up. So we returned by Betley to see Wrinehill and Heley Castle and could not see them for it rained heavily.

Staffordshire is lamentably lacking of histories. There are fine old halls at Audley and Betley, but I cannot find any mention of them in any book. The date that some one has painted on the ruined hall of Audley is probably taken from a charter of Henry III., confirming many lordships or manors to Henry de Alditheleighe in 1227. The charter mentions a new hall, but this Henry de Audeley, who had great estates, built a castle at Heley and got a license for a market at Betley, or Bettelegh as it was then spelt. The hall at Audley may have been rebuilt about 1540 as it bears another date.

The first mention of the name that I find was Liulf de Aldithelee, who murdered Gamel, son of Griffith, thane of Betley. Gamel was a common name with the Saxons or English, but Griffith is British or Welsh, and many Audleys in after years were slain by the Welsh. The blood-feud probably lasted, for the high ley on its steep hill became a border fortress.

It seemed impossible to make a photograph of the effigy in the darkness of Audley church, but X managed it as usual. My eye caught the eternal holy fire that burns before the altar as soon as we entered by the western door, and I soon missed the tablet on the wall in memory of Sam Woolf that I had copied years ago. An inscription on brass below the figure of a knight puzzled me a deal while the photograph was taking. It is on the ground, in a dark corner, in Norman French and black letter crowded together.

IN AUDLEY CHURCH

I made out that it was the grave of Sir Thomas d'Audeley, lord of Heley and Redcastle, a brother of Sir James d'Audeley; that he died in 1385, and ended

THE EFFIGY OF SIR JOHN DELVES, ONE OF THE SQUIRES

with the prayer that God on his soul might have mercy.

Afterwards, I found this Sir Thomas Audeley was second cousin to our Sir James, K.G., and son, not brother to another Sir James. As any Norman brass is rare in our district, I copy the following from Erdeswick:—

> Ici gist mons Thom's d'Audeley chiualer fra mons James d'Audele seigno' de helegh de rouge chastell q'i morult le XXXV de Januar l'an de gre' MCCCLXXXV qui vit de q'i alme dieu p'sa pite eit merci Amen

From the figures of the knights at Audley it was plain to see the armour shown on the statues at Doddington was the armour of a much later date, probably of the time when the hall was erected. They are there shown in Elizabethan ruffs and beards, with plenty of hair but very little top to their heads. They have swords and some plate armour. One of them carries a heart in his hand—perhaps it was meant for his own and he was taking it to the Holy Land. The effigy of Sir John Delves at Audley reminded me of that of Sir Hugh Calveley at Bunbury, and made me wish to see any other contemporary one, therefore I wrote at once to the Earl of Crewe for leave to photograph Sir Robert Fowleshurst, whose effigy is locked up in the Crewe chapel of Barthomley.

Here is another instance of the buyers of an estate buying the bodies of the ancestors of the sellers of the estate and having some other fellow's ancestors for their private property.

The requisite permission was given at once and the Major Domo, or whatever he may be, drove from Crewe Hall to open the chapel for us. The effigy of Sir Robert is in excellent preservation and very similar to those mentioned above, and also to that of their General, the Black Prince, at Canterbury. The long moustache falls outside the camail, or mail armour that protects the neck and shoulders. On the forehead the band of the basinet has letters engraven on it. Those on the right side and nearest to the light are J. H. S. or J. H. C., and on the other side I think they are a contraction of

THE EFFIGY OF SIR ROBERT FOWLESHURST IN FULL PANOPLY OF WAR ALL READY FOR BATTLE WITH HIS FOREHEAD GRAVEN 1650 ᛘᛆᚱᛁᛒᚤᚠᛅ

Nazarene. There is the collar of S. S. The misericordia dagger for putting foes out of their misery, is by his side, but the sword is gone. Perhaps the neighbouring farmers took the sword as they took that of Sir Hugh Calveley and ground it to powder for a charm, or cure of the footrot in their sheep. There are many pagan fetishes lingering still in our country.

This effigy of Sir Robert is probably a likeness of him in full panoply of war. His nose is rather worn down, and the mail looks like a curly beard. The Black Prince left orders that he was to have on his tomb an image of himself with his visage, "armed in steel all ready for battle." His soldier, Sir Robert, is shown here armed "from head to heel in Milan steel" all ready for battle, waiting the trumpet call, and on his forehead is the name of Jesus.

On this our second journey to Barthomley the sun shone so brightly X determined to take other photographs of the church and village inn, although those he had taken previously, when the weather was dull, had already gone for reproduction; but first we must take Sir Robert—and then came a storm. We sheltered in the inn instead of taking it. The hours went by and the rain came in torrents with thunder and lightning almost incessant. We tried lunch and then tea, treated Lord Crewe's men and sat in the snug, talked to anybody and everybody, waited for hours and at last went off in the wet to find that at home, only thirty miles away, there had been no rain all day—another proof of the wisdom of staying at home.

Lord Crewe's men had put the horse up at the rectory, but they naturally wanted refreshment at the inn. Their talk would have suited Thackeray. The coachman always addressed the old man with the keys as Mister; and the old man promptly contradicted everything he said, and called him Chawles. If Chawles ventured to tell of the delights of hunting where there

REMNANT OF SCREEN IN THE CHURCH OF THE MASSACRE

On it, but of later date are the words—
"Let there be no strife for we be brethren."

were miles of turf and one had nothing to do but "sit in the saddle and let 'em go," he was told his lordship was going to sell all his horses off and keep no more. Then Chawles might begin again: "Well, you know, Mister," but the old man would cut in—"No I don't, Chawles; you can't tell me what I know; I know too much already. Her leddyship always said to me—says she—'Don't talk of his ludship's affairs,' says she. 'No, your leddyship,' says I. Says she to me—she says—now Chawles do let me get a word in. Her leddyship thinks a lot o' me and she always says—says she"—&c. &c.

I could have told them a tale that was told to me fifty years ago about the host of that very inn, but as the present tenants may be his descendants I kept quiet and will tell it now, merely premising that the house bears the initials O. H., is dated 1614, and is believed to have always been an inn. It had to be propped up when we were there, as if it were soaked in its own liquor, but it is still The White Lion of Barthomley.

In the days when the clerk of the church kept the village inn and his feudal tenure or polygenous duties comprised the carting of his rector's coals, he went to Audley coal-pits for a load of coal, and took a barrel of ale with him. He would naturally be fresh, and he was persuaded to have more, was taken down the coal-pit when the drink had overcome him, and there he was left in the darkness. When his muddled senses returned and the colliers gibed at him, he cried aloud: "Oh please, good master devils, don't hurt me. I never hurted nobody. When I was on earth I was clerk of Barthomley; now I'm what you please." As he was only drunk and kept an ale-house when he was on earth they let him loose.

This was the second time the rain had spoiled our pilgrimages to the homes of the four squires. We had not found the Hall of Wrinehill, or Wrineford, where Sir

THE WHITE LION, BARTHOMLEY

John Hawkstone came from, though I well remember my father showing me an old house near to a large pool below the railway viaduct at Betley and saying that was Wrinehill Hall. Many things happen in fifty years, but I had never found my way there, and was not very likely to find it, for there is only a cart-track for nearly half a mile, and underneath the railway the slutch would be six inches deep. Pilgrims suffer hardships gladly—if they get their reward, and we were not much disappointed. We found an enormous farm-yard with a venerable gateway in the middle. On the other side of a large pool of water, that is fringed with reeds and less than it was in days gone by, there is a small mill and a big house not very old. I could not make the gateway fit the house for the breadth of the pool was between them. The farmer came to see what we were after, so I asked him if we might photograph the stone columns. His reply was something like, "Oh aye, but what's the good of fortygraffink them things, they're nobbut owd rubbitch. One o' them stone balls fell a bit sin and did mak' such a hole i' th' muck. If yo wanten some ut to fortygraf, tak' ma young bull—that would be a pictur'—he's a bonny beast—he is so. Pedigree bred? Rather! Twelve months old last Valentine's Day middle o' th' neet."

We learnt that only a few years since there stood by this gateway two enormous walnut trees. One was struck by lightning and the other felled as some one offered £7, 10s. 0d. for it. But after it had been felled it was found to be not sound in the heart, and the buyer "rued bargain and wouldn'r a' it." The old hall has utterly vanished. Our new friend told us he had plowed its site and set it with potatoes. Fancy the dust of the knightly families of Hawkstones and Egertons becoming potatoes! It may be the best use that could be made of it.

The rent notes for the estate are in the name of the

ALL THAT IS LEFT OF WRINEHILL HALL

Earl of Wilton "and others," and the descent of the estate as shown by the Egerton pedigree is rather interesting.

The great-grandson of Sir John Hawkstone was Hugh de Eggerton of Wrynhill, Esquire, who built himself a new Hall on the small estate (elsewhere named the

THE PRIDE OF WRINEHILL

Wryne or Wrineford). The Egertons stuck to the place with the tenacity of the family, and about two hundred years after Hugh, Sir John Egerton of Wrinehill married an heiress, Elizabeth Holland of Heaton and Denton, near Manchester. Sir John died at Wrinehill, but his progeny built Heaton Hall and his great-grandson was the first Earl of Wilton.

The recent purchase by the Corporation of Manchester of Heaton Hall and its square mile of park is well known. The sale by auction of its contents produced some sensational prices (for instance the dining-room chairs as related in my last book). But there were many family portraits and large pieces of furniture that were not offered for sale, and some time after a dealer in antiquities told me these things were all to be sold quietly and quickly at the Coal Exchange. He thought there was something strange about it, and I went at once to the Town Clerk to suggest these were fixtures sold with the Hall and the property of the city. Our Town Clerk said there was no proof of that. I replied that in any case the Corporation could have the lot for a small sum in settlement. My colleagues would not trouble about it. They look upon me as merely an antiquary, that is one who is afflicted with a harmless form of lunacy, not fit to be a city councillor, to go on deputations and make speeches about economy and keeping down the rates.

There was very little notice of the sale, and many things were knocked down dirt cheap to brokers, who resold most of the family portraits to X for as many pounds as they had given shillings, though a Raeburn went off to London at once. Soon after we had been to Wrinehill X came quite jubilant to tell me that among his Heaton Hall portraits were two in carved oak frames of Sir John Egerton of Wrinehill and Elizabeth Holland his wife, bearing their names, signed and dated "Kneller pinxit, 1687."

He set to work at once to photograph them but found that as usually happens with old oil paintings, the faded yellows and browns take as if they were black, that is, they do not show at all in the photograph. Sir John was exposed for more than an hour before his yellow wig or hair would show itself; but here he is at last, as self-satisfied as the young bull that is the pride of Wrinehill at the present day.

76 PILGRIMAGES TO OLD HOMES

The grand home of the Earls of Wilton in its spacious park at Heaton has now become the play-

SIR JOHN EGERTON OF WRINEHILL

Sir John acquired, *jure uxoris*, Heaton and other estates near Manchester, and the citizens of Manchester bought Heaton Hall from one who was probably a descendant in the seventeenth generation of Sir John Hawkstone of Wrinehill, one of the four squires.

ground of the dwellers in the slums of Manchester. Socialism is triumphant. Music for the masses is paid for out of the rates. Dancing on the greensward is

HEATON HALL

free to all, and the grand "Adam" mantelpiece in the hall is hidden behind piles of bottles of pop.

ELIZABETH HOLLAND

As the picture bears her maiden name as wife of Sir John Egerton, it was probably a wedding present, and possibly from the tenantry.

As We, the People, have now possession of the estate we naturally want pedigrees with blue-blooded ancestors and other emoluments, therefore I told X that he certainly ought to have Audley and the four squires for ancestors. He worked with a will on pedigrees, and portraits, and ponderous tomes, until he had got the lot, if not lineal, as ancestors collateral. The term is good though the details are voluminous and wearisome. I need no pedigree to make me feel they are my "ancestors collateral." They were neighbours, and their families intermarried and have been breeding with their neighbours for more than five hundred years. My forefathers, who never came from anywhere, but who simply grew there or thereabouts, must have had some primitive ancestor before church registers were invented.

We wandered on a little further to find the ruins of Heley, or Helegh, Castle on its conical rock. An exceedingly deep moat has been cut out of the solid rock all round it, and the site is now overgrown with trees and nettles. From it there is a grand view of many miles of fertile country. It was doubtless built to overawe the Welsh and push them further back, for a neighbouring hill still keeps its Celtic name of Bryn—but we must leave these devious border wanderings and the tale of the four squires if we are ever to end the tale of the house of Delves.

Sir John Delves was succeeded by his brother, Sir Henry, whose great-grandson, another Sir John, was killed in the Wars of the Roses at Tewksbury. His son, another John, was one of those who took refuge from the battle in the abbey church, whose sanctuary even the fiery young King Edward IV. dare not violate; but he bided his time, till fair words and hunger caused the fugitives to trust him, and then off went their heads.

That was the time when Merry England saw its King Edward stab, with his own hand and in cold blood, his rival, Edward, Prince of Wales.

Sir John Delves and his son John were buried at

"STABBED AT TEWKSBURY" 79

Tewksbury, but afterwards taken to Wybunbury, where their effigies lay on a gorgeous tomb inscribed with their names and titles, and ending with the prayer that on

COTTAGE AT HELEY

their souls there might be mercy. Men have had no more mercy on their tomb and effigies than others had on their bodies, for all have vanished.

It is one of the sarcasms of history that only in the times of war, when men are killing one another, we find

FROM THE RUINS OF HELEY

any history. I find very little history of Dodington Castle from the time it was built after the great French War until our Civil War, when Malbon's diary tells us Dodington Hall was besieged by the King's army on the 4th of January 1643-4. "Captyn Harwar for the p'liam^t with about 100 men well Armed and provisioned, and Magazen sufficiente for a fortnight ... depted awaye onelie with theire app'ell and went to Wem, not being suffred to come to Namptwiche." But the triumph of the Royalists was short. "Uppon Wednesdaye the vii of ffebruary 1643-4 Dodington Hall beinge kepte by the Kinge's p'tie was assaulted by Namptwiche forces and upon some Shott with theire greate ordnance ... the howse was deliu'ed up ... left behind almost twoe hundred Armes and good store of victualls, powder, matches, and Bulletts."

Then Prince Rupert came "plu'dring all the Countrey ... some of his men were Slayne as they passed alonge by Dodington where there were in the Hall about fourtie Soldyers for the p'liam^t."

Of the Sir Thomas Delves of that time I find no record in the war. He was an old man and probably on the side of the Parliament. The Hall was protected by a moat and also joined on to the Castle, which, fortunately, still stands to-day with its four squires on guard. Without them the Castle would have gone the way of all the rest. The moat is dry and levelled and the Hall is gone. Another Hall, ugly and classical, like most of its day, was built in 1790 by the great-grandfather of the present lord, Sir Delves L. Broughton, Bart.

Two generations further back the only surviving child and heiress of Sir Thomas Delves had become the wife of Sir Brian Broughton of Broughton Hall in Staffordshire, a charming old house about ten miles further south than Doddington, and known to me from boyhood as it is only two miles from Standon Hall.

ON THE WAY TO DODDINGTON

Let us begin our pilgrimage at Crewe, where one of the squires came from. We soon see the grand

WESTERN DOOR OF WYBUNBURY CHURCH

tower of Wybunbury, the parish church of Doddington; Doddington itself being only a township with a population of fifty-six persons a short time since, and probably they dwelt in the Hall or thereabouts. In childhood's days I often heard of the leaning tower of Wybunbury, and have a dim recollection of seeing it. This splendid tower did lean over to the north-east, being five feet from perpendicular, but the foundation on the other side was gradually undermined and some of the stone sawn through, time after time, until the tower straightened itself.

The church is new, the old one having mostly tumbled into its own vaults. The effigies of the Delves of Tewksbury are gone, but there is a brass to their heir, who was the son of the one and brother to the other.

Here lyeth Rafe Dellups Esquyer of Dodenton and Batheryn hys Wyfe . . . MCCCCC and IXI3 on whose Sowllys Allmyghty Jhu have mercy.

There may have been other monuments to the Delves family in prior years, for I should think the once great church of Wybunbury was partly built from the spoils of the French, as Bunbury grew over the magnificent tomb of Sir Hugh Calveley.

Instead of beautiful Gothic altar-tombs with mailed effigies there is a hideous, cumbrous, Jacobean thing that X would photograph. It is in remembrance of Sir Thomas Smith, whose wife, Anne Smith, "gave him this monument." His hair and moustaches are luxuriant enough to have been growing ever since he was born and after he was dead; and over his effigy are proudly displayed the emblazoned arms with the numerous quarterings of the great family of Smith, one of the aristocratic families whose ancestors came over with the Conqueror.

From the churchyard may be seen many acres of the rich land of Cheshire, the quaint little village on the hill-side, the old fashioned "pub" at the church gates, the dower house of the Delves family known as The Cliff, and on the next hill the alms-house or school inscribed with the name of Delves.

As many do not know what it is to delve, I may

be pardoned the following little tale. Fifty years ago our country doctor, who was a busy man with good

THE GORGEOUS MONUMENT OF SIR TOM SMITH

horses, knowing all the bridle paths, the best apple trees, and the good gardens, advertised for a groom. A very smart gentleman's-servant applied for the place. The doctor asked him, "Can you delve any?" The man did not understand. The doctor explained, "Can you delve? Can you dig in the garden?" "Not me, sir," said the man. "Good morning, sir."

The arms of the Delves family bear allusion to the name in three black turves, or spadefuls of turf, as cut to-day in our local mosses at one delve.

Our road onwards from Wybunbury becomes more undulating and beautiful. At the first gates of Doddington there lately stood a fine old black and white house, known as the Boar's Head, but it has been rebuilt in the fashion of the day. Further on are many picturesque cottages that tempted us to tarry on our way. An old woman begged us to photograph her cat. If the disreputable looking beast with its scratched face had been in my garden, I should have been willing to do something, but it went after the birds, and another, a quieter one, came, and is shown in the picture sitting placidly under a gooseberry bush, though two women were cackling at it all the time.

We cycled about the park, photographed the Castle, and dawdled time away, hoping that some one would come to see what we were doing, and then we might ask questions; but nobody came, and the birds chattered at us, for the remnant of the Castle appears to be railed round and left for the birds. Its upper chambers, with their broken windows, should be an ideal home for owls. The cuckoo's call came from the neighbouring garden, where, perhaps, he was searching the gooseberry bushes for caterpillars, and slowly we walked across the park, skirting the wilder part where the red deer dwell, until we came to the London road.

Then is the long ascent to Woore where the three counties join, and down three roads we may roll along Staffordshire, Shropshire, or Cheshire. The middle one is our way for Broughton, but we shall not be in Shropshire long, for, by the picturesque old houses shown, we come to Mucklestone. That is in Staffordshire, is part of the Crewe estates, and from its tower Queen

THE DELVES DOWER HOUSE, WYBUNBURY

THE WAY TO DODDINGTON

THE WAY TO DODDINGTON

Margaret watched the Wars of the Roses on Blore-heath, and saw her commander-in-chief, another Lord Audley, left dead on the field while her army melted away.

The school is "loosing," and education being the burning question of the day, X asks me about "church atmosphere" here. How I laughed at the thoughts of my childhood and the tales of it that he had forgotten. It was here my father's sister's husband was a school-

master and farmer at Mucklestone Wood, and churchwarden for many years, a tall, handsome, and polite old man, who could curse till every one was dazed and shrivelled. He consigned us all to eternal damnation on a "sacrament" Sunday because we should be late for church and he had to get the "sacrament things" ready. What does X mean by "church atmosphere"? Is it any part of a sound, religious education? For that, my uncle laboured when he tried to drive the catechism into the little brutes; to teach them to submit themselves to their pastors and masters, to be lowly and reverent to all their betters—

"'Tis education forms the common mind
And with the birch we drive it in behind."

THE HOME OF SERFS OF DODDINGTON

DORRINGTON

BEARSTONE

Don't I remember the words of the psalmist and the reverend gentleman's hand, for rheumatism or bad temper had clenched and stiffened his fingers at various angles till we did not know what he was hitting us with.

It reminds me of an Irishman who was asked if he had ever been struck by lightning, and replied he did not know. He was told he must know if he had been struck by lightning, but he persisted in his denial, and at last impatiently explained: "Shure if ye'd only been wed a week or two ye'd ne'er know what it was as had shtrucken ye."

"Church atmosphere"! It is strange any one should ask me about it at Mucklestone. The finest bilberries anywhere grown are in the Burnt Woods and the Forty Acres, but under any and every bush there might be that old serpent the devil in the form of a very lively adder. Did a cow cast her calf, or a sheep get maggoty, you should have heard the churchwarden curse the witchcraft that had bewitched them. The powers of evil were everywhere, even on my pet ducks, for if they made their nests by the pit-side the fox would take them, or if their ducklings swam on the water the pike from below would grab them. When the cows gave bloody milk I was unjustly accused of taking a swallow's nest, but when the milk was sour ranters must have been psalm-singing.

There were countless happy days and memories, but the cloud on them was the intense narrowness of the schoolmaster-churchwarden. Yet I honestly doubt, even now, whether any board-school or higher education has taught any one to make bilberry pudding with thick suety paste as good as my poor aunt made it; or to make bread as sweet as the sweet yellow bread she made in a brick oven heated with boughs of pine. A roast hare, stuffed with bread-crumbs and suet, seasoned with parsley, sweet marjoram and thyme, basted with cream and served with sauce of liver and cream, was food fit for the heathen gods. It would bring water in the mouth of a saint.

BEARSTONE

MUCKLESTONE CHURCH

Even England's famous roast beef can rarely be gotten anywhere now. Meat is baked in an oven and as dry as the baker's bread at two days old. The modern Professors of Technical Instruction teach their novel-loving pupils that it is more economical in time, trouble, and coal to bake—they call it to cook—their meat in an oven. The consequent insipidity and indigestion drives them to doctors who say they suffer from dyspepsia and give them pills. They think they know better than Moses who laid down the law that the lamb without blemish for the Passover was to be roast with fire, not sodden with the steam in an oven. What has the roasting of beef to do with education? What is education? My Staffordshire aunts always denounced it, were excellent cooks, good housewives, healthy and happy to old age. There are two of them living, one in her ninety-sixth year, the other in her eighty-sixth year; lively and talkative still. I remember them with gratitude, but not the schoolmaster-churchwarden. X asks what about "church atmosphere" here! How can he appreciate it? I may again reply in the words of the psalmist: "Why do the people imagine a vain thing?"

What would the atmosphere be like when the boy forgot his catechism and lost his gravy? A scholar from a distance brought his dinner in a basin tied up in a cloth, but he had words with another scholar, and to use his own words, "Dicky Benion give me some of his lip so I clouted him o'er 'is 'ed wi' th' basson and I lost a' my gravy." The basin broke, for Dicky Benion's head was thicker and harder than it and the good gravy was wasted on his hair.

The rector is the son of the man who was rector here sixty years ago. He is said to be as good a judge of a horse as of a sermon. The roses from the battlefield of Blore-heath that came mingled red and white from the commingled blood of our forefathers, where brothers killed brothers in a quarrel they knew

BROUGHTON HALL

DOORWAY OF BROUGHTON HALL

nothing about, bloom in our garden now. These sweet mementoes of the wars of York and Lancaster have ever been, and still are, cherished by us, though I have taken office under the red rose and set the badge aloft in the stained glass of my library window.

The blacksmith at the forge by the church in my enchanted childhood's days was Skelhorn, the descend-

BROUGHTON CHURCH
"Where heaves the turf in many a mouldering heap."

ant in tailmale of the smith who reversed the shoes on Queen Margaret's horses when the battle was lost and won four centuries ago Toryism might well be rampant, but my uncle straightens his six-foot figure no more as he gloats over the torments that are to come on the next generation, for long ago they buried him—the first burial in a field then added to the old churchyard of Mucklestone; and with him ended most of my childhood's fears of another Bonaparte, another Revolution, the imminent burning up of the earth

THE FIREPLACE IN THE HALL, BROUGHTON

and all that is therein, and the terror of the fires of hell for ever.

Over Ashley Heath, by the Loggerheads Inn, and through the Burnt Woods we come to Broughton in Staffordshire. The place consists of a hall and a church. The only bit of history that I can find is in Erdeswick, where a charter of Edward I. mentions Roger

AN UNRESTORED CHURCH

de Napton, who had issue Elias de Broughton and ten generations. Their feudal duties were to plow in winter, to reap in harvest, and to keep ward at Eccleshall Castle for their overlords—the diet of a man being then valued at half-a-penny a day. The church is one of the best kept—unrestored and unmolested—little churches that I know. I painted a picture of it fifty years ago, and it looks just the same as it did then excepting for a white cross that some one has put up like the stock article of suburban cemeteries. There may have been more burials than one in the fifty years, but perhaps the other parties, the buried and the buriers, have been content with the green grass—under the sod, the sweetly scented, slowly mouldering sod.

THE BACK STAIRS, BROUGHTON HALL

The Hall is dated 1639, and the initials T. B. over the front door stand for Thomas Broughton the builder, who had been High Sheriff of the county. His son, or grandson, would be the Sir Brian Broughton who married the heiress of the Delves of Doddington

THE STAIRS, BROUGHTON HALL

THE STAIRWAY

and with their descendants the estates have descended unto this day.

The Hall was built in a troublous time at the beginning of the great Civil War, and was made with a remarkable hiding-hole—a fair-sized room with no window or aperture but a passage that branched from the main chimney flue. It seems to me that all access to this room would be cut off if the fire in the Hall were lighted. To get into this hidden chamber a man would have to climb up steps in the chimney

THE HALL TABLE

for eighteen feet, then go down a dark passage groping his way and patiently wait in the silence and gloom of the grave. If a fire was lighted after the fugitive had got safely into the secret room the smoke should ascend the chimney flue, but if the chimney 'smoked' it might be very uncomfortable. The room has now become a smoking-room with a window and stairs of its own.

The handsome staircase in the Hall does not show itself in the photograph as well as it should, and we do not attempt to give a picture of the Flemish stained glass in the hall window, though it is dated 1651, for the lady of the house showed us the figure of a rabbi about to operate with a fearful pair of scissors.

We are told the outside of the house is of timber-work, very ornamental, but unfortunately covered with plaster. The corbels are carved into the

OLD GLASS IN BROUGHTON CHURCH

likeness of birds and beasts, and probably there are quatrefoils in black and white hidden behind the stucco.

Roundabout, in beautiful, undulating parkland, are fine old trees and a gem of a little church that is good enough to have inspired Gray's "Elegy."

UNDER THE CEDAR AT BUERTON HALL.

110 PILGRIMAGES TO OLD HOMES

Quickly flies the time in these quiet, rural spots, and more than once we had promised to wander on to call on kindred who were young some forty years ago, but are grand-parents now, and we find them quietly resting in the eventide under the cedar at Buerton Hall.

THE DAYLIGHT DIES

THE LAND OF CASTLES

BRECON TO PEMBROKE

EVER since our romantic pilgrimage up the pass in the Eglwyseg mountains to the World's End, where the fair Nesta was hidden after her abduction from Pembroke Castle and the flight across Wales, it had been our wish to some day go on pilgrimage to see the stately Norman fortress of Pembroke that was fired by the wild Welshman on its night of revelry, so that in the tumult he might seize the lady of the Castle and her children.

By the southern train through Shrewsbury, so often used before, we found the ancient town of Abergavenny (or Abergenny usually called). Here are famous monuments in the church, and outside the station I asked the way. "Which church?" was the answer given. I said, "The old church," but the local free-born Briton knew nothing about the age of the churches. "Which is the way to the old church?" I asked again. "Straight on," was the reply. "But there are two roads bending left and right; which is it?" "I won't tell ye any more. Ye can go down as many roads as ye like," was the next answer, and X said we were not in Wales, so I thought we must be on the way to Ireland.

We found the church, and with some trouble got the key, but the parson was from home, and there were doubts about photographing, therefore X would not take anything (though the monuments of the Herberts were exceedingly fine), because another parson had lately been very rude to him for photographing in a church without permission; so every reader of this book has missed some pictures, and the damp church was locked up again probably until the next Sunday, when there would be service and a collection.

In drizzly rain we soon tired of Abergenny and sought the road for Brecon, the first stage of the long cycling in our pilgrimage to the furthest corner of Wales. The country round the valley of the Usk

CRICKHOWELL CASTLE

was like to that about the English Lakes—country seats in parks with giant trees and sloping hills behind, with a river rushing by instead of calmer lake. The weather cleared, and our spirits rose as we gradually ascended into purer air and looked for tea at Crickhowell, where we photographed our first castle, but left the great gate or Porth Mawr because it was not picturesque, though local patriotism thinks it grand.

At Tretower, which is a few miles further, and down a by-lane, we find a round tower, now in ruins,

TRETOWER CASTLE

rising from a circling moat in pleasant pastoral country where the cuckoo calls, and carefully we turn our bits of money over glad to hear the welcome sound again and feel our luck is mending. Here is something picturesque enough as the evening sun gleams through the mists and lights up colours that our photographs can never take. Carefully and warily a gander and a goose lead thirteen little goslings to the water of the moat, and we have to hurry before the reflections are spoilt.

Then comes a long hill, up which we have to tramp. The country round grows wilder, and the scene down the vale of Usk is very grand. The mountains are higher, and we become weary as we toil up the steep ascent of the Bwlch, but the cutting through the top of the pass is reached, and then follows a grand roll down miles towards Brecon.

The Castle of Brecon Hotel is a noted hostelry, and dinner was ready. Oxtail soup, not made from tabloids, but from sections of the tails of well-fed cattle. Pink and speckled trout from the river flowing past the windows, where we could see a patient angler at his work. Was he catching some for us? The waitress said he was, so we bespoke some more for breakfast on the morrow.

Early in the morning we were ready for the trout, and the fisherman was still in the river, though we do not know that he had been there all night; he is in the photograph, a speck in the distance under the second arch from the left:—

> "Patient at morn, at evening patient still
> Peace have they if not fish—and peace is best."

Our waitress greeted us with saying it was a charming morning; but when I asked how that could be, as it was thickly drizzling rain, she replied she did not know it was wet. "Then why say it's charm-

THE BRIDGE OVER THE USK AT BRECON

ing?" "Oh, I always tell visitors it's a charming morning, to put them in good humour for their breakfast." Then the charmer cut up half a loaf and threw it on the lawn for a flock of villainous daws and rooks; no respectable bird could get a crumb. She asked if we were much troubled with radicals in our country, and I told her my friend X was a frightful radical. With great commiseration she said, "Oh, I'm so sorry. We are much troubled with radicals here. They want to have a Scotchman for chief constable. Just fancy! In Wales. But they shan't. Ours is a dear man. You saw him when you went to bed?" "Yes, and heard him for hours," said X. "If the chief makes that noise, what do the others do?" "They would make more noise," I replied; "for the chief is chosen as being the most virtuous of all the constables; that is understood, and folk-lore tells us that any good mother devotes her best unto the service of the Lord. Therefore her biggest son, especially if he does not like work, becomes a parson or a Bobby."

Brecon is a quaint old-fashioned town with some history, a ruined castle in the garden of the hotel where the stream of Honddhu joins the Usk, a great church on the hill, a fine bridge across the angler's famous salmon-river, hills all round rising to the picturesque peaks of the Beacons, which we dimly see through misty rain as impatiently we long for better weather. All things come to those who can wait, and, after strolling up and down the quiet little town with its narrow unpaved streets, the mists ascend, and we venture to photograph and then journey on.

History says the Castle of Brecknock was built by Bernard the Norman, one of the many husbands of Nesta, the aforesaid ancestress of X. But in this case she complained to the King, who was partly another husband, that her son was not Bernard's son, and therefore he lost the estates. Her matrimonial engagements were rather complicated, and there were more women than one of the name, so perhaps there is some mistake and we should always hope for the best.

THE CASTLE, BRECON

Giraldus tells us that in Llanvaes Church (by Brecon) a boy was robbing a pigeon's nest, when his fingers stuck to the stone for three days while his parents prayed hard, and the finger marks are there to this day; but we had no time to look for them.

Charles Kemble, the actor, and his sister, Mrs. Siddons, were born in Brecon; also the Duke of Buckingham, who owned the Castle in the days of his friend Richard III., and, getting snubbed by that Anointed of the Lord, is reported by Shakspere to have said:

> "Oh! let me be gone
> To Brecknock while my fearful head is on."

He went there and talked to a prisoner, the Bishop of Ely, our Cheshire Morton, who gave the King the good strawberries in Holborn. So the Duke conspired with the Bishop, and the end came as might be expected. The Duke was beheaded and the Bishop became Archbishop.

But a better known Shaksperean hero than either of them came from Brecon, that is Davy Gam, the son of a Llewelyn, known as Fluellen. He did wonders at Agincourt, persuaded the King to wear a leek, made the braggart Pistol eat his leek, and when the King, after the great victory, said, "God fought for us," Fluellen replied, "Yes, my conscience, He did us great good."

Plain history says he received the nickname of Gam because his eyes were "gammy," and his neighbours called him "a squinting, red-haired knave." Glyndwr burnt his house because he had sought to kill Glyndwr, and before that he had slain a big man in the High Street of Brecon. He fought valiantly at Agincourt, was knighted there by Henry, whose life he had saved in the battle, and there he died. It is also said that he or his son-in-law, Vaughan of Tretower, were the authors of the saying anent the French host that "there were enough to kill, enough to take prisoners, and enough to run away."

In the Priory Church is an oaken effigy of a lady in Elizabethan costume with ruff on neck, which is

ABERBRAN

said to be the likeness of the wife of one of the Games, or Gams, of Aberbran about 1555. As some one has knocked off the lady's nose and top lip, her beauty is rather spoilt, but the effigy is worth noting, and also a curious pentagonal oaken sideboard in a corner of the church having two sides to the walls and three in front. It is a noble cruciform church, with fine triplet lancet windows at the eastern end, but hidden and crowded by big forest trees, one being a venerable hollow oak. When Leland wrote of the river Usk he spelt it Uiske, but sometimes he lapsed into Wiske. I wonder what he was thinking of?

Onward we go for the pass over the hills and the watershed by Trecastle for Llandovery. Unfortunately we miss one old house of the Gams, but photograph another at Aberbran. There were two mares with foals and two cows with calves in the field when we stopped to take this very picturesque old home, but the camera scared the mares away, and one cow moved out of the picture, although two calves are there.

At Llanspyddyd Church there are yew trees, perhaps the finest we ever saw. I sat like old Mortality on the roots of one to give some idea of the size of the bole. No idea of their height could be given. They were higher than the church and of enormous girth; the biggest we could not take. These yews may be venerable patriarchs indeed, for Brychan, the prince or chief after whom the country is named, was buried here, and some cross or stone commemorates him. He was a saint because he was the son of a saint, and he had about fifty children that he knew of, and they would all be saints according to one of the interesting customs of the country.

For many miles we steadily rise uphill, passing through a fertile country with fine views, for all the land lies high.

At the mountain village of Trecastle the Castle is

gone, though its mound remains, and the manor-house has become an inn. Down the vale of the Gwydderig we descend about six hundred feet in six miles, having left the watershed of the Usk for the descent of the Towy. The distance between Brecon and Llandovery has been a puzzle to me all day, for no two books or folk agree. To the best of my recollection we pass a half-way house or inn, stated to be half-way between Trecastle and Llandovery and five miles to the latter. The next milestone says six miles to Llandovery, or I thought it did, though the free-wheeling was too good to stop. The others were certainly at variance. On the other side of the town the milestones again were wrong, and I wondered whether the natives caught their mendacious habits from the milestones, or the milestones theirs from the natives. Hard, grey milestones certainly lied without blushing as they stared fixedly at us, and my hind tyre burst with a bang as if in indignation at them.

Llandovery, the church of the waters, where three streams meet, is apparently kept alive by its cattle-market, for when there are no cattle there seems nothing alive about the place. We crossed the wide and empty market-place to the Castle Hotel, where we had difficulty in finding any one. The ruined castle was all there was to photograph, but something should be said of our hostel, for it was the scene of the conversion of Llandovery's famous Vicar.

Rees Pritchard was a native, born about 1575, educated at Oxford, a wild, drunken young man, into whose care was committed the cure of the souls of the parish. Into the Castle Inn, where he was drinking, there walked a goat, a favourite, tame old Billy. He and his companions for mischief let the goat drink all the ale it would, and the goat got drunk, staggered, and fell, and there it lay all night. The Vicar was taken home in a wheel-barrow, but returned to his

LLANSPYDDYD CHURCHYARD

shame in the morning. Again he offered the goat more ale, but the beast shook its head and would have none. "Oh, my God," said the Vicar, "has the beast more sense than I?" and he never tasted intoxicants again. He wrote hymns and composed tunes for them, the work well known through Wales as *Canwyll y Cymry* or the "Welshman's Candle." On this spot, three

LLANDOVERY CASTLE

hundred years ago, was the candle lighted that has been a blessing to thousands.

From Llandovery we cycled down the vale of Towy in a lovely country. Here and there, by the almost hidden river, were large beds of shingle, greyish white, water-worn stones, showing what the winters' storms could do. On either side rose wooded hills, and the cattle looked well liking. It was very pleasant travelling, and the village of Llanwrda looked most picturesque, but soon there came the burst tyre, and at Llangadock we took the train for Llandilo, a few miles further, where we had intended to stay for the night.

After an early dinner I asked the landlord if we could walk to the lonely mountain fortress of Cerrig Cennen. He said it was scarcely possible on that evening, but a customer, who lived near to the place, was then in the hotel, would shortly be driving home, and would be glad of our company. It was very difficult to persuade X to trespass on the kindness of a stranger and trust himself in the gig of some one returning from market, but we did make the venture and enjoyed it exceedingly, although our host and charioteer could talk very little English at the best of times.

After various delays and much unintelligible talk while the daylight was fading, we started and went fairly well for about a mile, then the way became very steep, and we wished to walk, but our friend would not allow it. He said the horse was a good one, worth £40 and would draw twice our weight up any hill if it took its time. So we all three sat in a row, huddled up, fat and easy, while the good horse plodded on, and our friend painfully pondered for words of English. We gradually learnt that it was impossible to photograph the precipitous rock and Castle of Cerrig Cennen, unless we had a gallows a hundred feet high. Nothing was known about the Castle; even men from Birmingham, who studied big books in big libraries, could find nothing, therefore we must be content with looking at it, unless we slept with our charioteer, perhaps three in a bed, and climbed to the Castle in the morning.

Nearly all the historical, topographical, and theological lore of our friend was lost for want of English. He was intensely patriotic; many times he told us the Welsh are a grand people. Oh, they are so: see how much money they make out of the English. Aye, and they save it! Save it! that's the rub. He said at last that X must be Welsh, though he had never heard of Nesta. We had to say good-bye in a most weird scene. High up in the mountains, we seemed to be above a sea of mist or cloud from which rose isolated peaks where the dying daylight lingered, though all below was dark. The ghostly ruins of Cerrig Cennen Castle were grey against the sky, as if its crag rose out of an abyss; and all around were other ghostly shapes further and further until all seemed melted into mist.

Then came the tramp downhill in the dark for miles towards the lights of Llandilo, and, without troubling ourselves about the famous code of laws of Howel dha, we went to bed.

In the morning a new tyre had to be put on my hind wheel to guard against accidents, and we cycled off towards Carmarthen, on a good road, through grand scenery; enormous trees showed the goodness of the land and climate. In places the roadside was gay with purple orchis, a flower rarely seen by me. Flowers were most luxuriant everywhere, and the vale of Towy certainly is fine.

Dryslwyn Castle reminds one of the castles on the Rhine. Crumbling ruins on a grassy mound that is almost a precipice down to a swiftly flowing river. The difficulty is to photograph castle and river on one plate. It is hopeless to get the windings of the stream through the wooded hills, and the twittering swallows or the rising fish. The sheep do show as dots on the green hillside, but many times I feel my words or X's pictures fail to portray even a fraction of the beautiful scenes through which we passed.

Dryslwyn Castle was taken by the English in September 1285. Seven hundred men were killed by a mined part of the Castle falling on them. An engine, hauled by sixty oxen, cast big stones against the Castle, and the besieging army were mostly Welsh allies or traitors.

Caermardyn, or the Caer of Merlin, on the Tywy, but now Carmarthen, was our next resting-place. It is a thorough Welsh town with narrow steep streets, high walls that are partly prison or remnant of castle, fine old church with monument of Sir Rhys ap Thomas, who, tradition says, slew Richard at Bosworth, the

DRYSLWYN CASTLE

place of the burning of the martyred Bishop of St. Davids, a noted inn called the Ivybush, a broad and rapid river where Britons fish from coracles, crowds of parsons and cattle, with many other things we wished to see : but we journeyed on by train for Tenby, tired of cycling and sight-seeing, and longing for a little rest.

We rested in the railway carriage, and remembered a friend who told me he once travelled towards Tenby, and, somewhere on the way about Carmarthen, the train stopped by fields dotted with mushrooms, while passengers, guard and engine-driver gathered as many mushrooms as they liked, and, after filling all their spare baskets or hat-boxes, the train carefully resumed its journey.

Our progress was so slow that, after consultation with the guard, we merely alighted at Tenby to send our little luggage to the hotel called Royal Gatehouse, while we went on by the train to Pembroke to see the Castle and country there and cycle back that evening, thinking we should thereby save almost a day.

We did save many hours, though we did two days work in one. The long railway journey from Carmarthen to Pembroke was restful to our muscles, but tiresome to our senses. The sea came into sight as we neared Tenby, and we skirted it for some miles, seeing Caldy Island, but not seeing the famous Castle of Manorbier, or Maenor Pyrr, where Giraldus was born. The land between the mountains and the sea was flat, green, and fertile, and in one part there was a large herd of the Castle Martin cattle.

The goal of this long pilgrimage across South Wales was to Pembroke Castle, that famous fortress in the little England beyond Wales. It may not be known to all, and therefore it is better to mention the fact, that the Norman conquerors of England settled in the extreme south-west of Wales, with Pembroke Castle for their chief stronghold, and brought many Flemings with their followers, who peopled the rocky coasts for centuries before the Welsh were driven back from parts of England.

In that corner, with help by sea, the Anglo-Flemish always kept their ground by unremitting war; and at this day the observant traveller may see the majority of the names of men and places are English, and the people themselves are not the darker Celts or British of the neighbouring hills.

PEMBROKE CASTLE

From here Strongbow conquered Ireland, and here Gerald de Windsor lived with Nesta and gave a great feast to his neighbours, when Owen fired the Castle to seize her in the tumult. How did he carry her over more than a hundred miles of mountains with rivers and morasses in between? Even the wild Welshmen had no wings, and there were no roads. The roads are few and bad enough in our time. Let any one consider what the country is like to-day between Pembroke and Plas Uchaf Eglwyseg in the World's End beyond Llangollen. We have gone over it now, X for love of Nesta, the Helen of Wales, the ancestress of myriads; and I for love of wandering on pilgrimage along our fatherland to see the homes in which our fathers or their so-called betters lived and died.

We were rather disappointed in some things about Pembroke Castle. The seaward side is magnificent, and access to the sea enormously added to its strength. The inside is bare and bald—a Norman stronghold built for war and nothing else but war. Here, if anywhere, men had to be ready by day and ready by night.

> "—they carved at the meal
> With gloves of steel
> And they drank the red wine through the helmet barred."

There may have been banqueting hall and chapel, but we saw them not, only the massive round tower of the keep and the impregnable gate-house. What there would be for Owen to fire is a mystery. I can only think of the rushes on the floor; they would make a great smoke, and the red wines of Gascony or Burgundy would add to the revels and probably my lady fair knew all about it, and wanted a little change, for two of her children and two of her husband's children were also taken. For those who wish to know more of the tale I would refer them to our pilgrimage to The World's End as recorded in my book of pilgrimages to Old Homes on the Welsh border, merely

THE FROWNING PORTAL, PEMBROKE CASTLE

transcribing a few lines: "In after years the Norman Earl and the Prince of Wales found themselves fighting on the same side, but sides and friends were tossed aside when they knew one another. The injured and the injurer, Norman Gerald and Welsh Owen, gripped in the fierce hate which death alone could end, and dare-devil Owen's last fight was fought."

Sadder tales than this have gathered round the

THE ROUND TOWER

blood-stained walls of Pembroke, and one by many centuries is nearer to our own time. In the Civil War and under the guidance of its Mayor, a Puritan named Poyer, Pembroke was a tower of strength on the side of Parliament all through the war, but near its close, for some inexplicable reason, Poyer turned with all his followers in defiance of Oliver and his Ironsides. Carlyle says he was confused with brandy and Presbyterian texts of Scripture. Famine and the lack of water starved them out, and ultimately three leaders were condemned to die. Then it was thought one victim should be enough,

PEMBROKE CASTLE

and lots were drawn. Three papers were put in a hat. On two of them, "Life given by God" was written. The third was blank. Poyer drew it and was shot.

"Rosemary, that's for remembrance." A fine bush of it stands at the porter's doorway by the Castle gate,

ONE OF THE OLD BREED

but no one knows in whose remembrance it grows. We have some tea amid the ruins, and fly for Lamphey, where is another ancient home—a ruined palace of St. Davids bishops.

Here, in old Llandyfei, is another remnant of wild cattle. They seem very like to those we fortunately saw at Chartley, as any one may see by comparing the photographs; for one old patriarch here allowed himself to be stalked.

A PALACE IN RUIN

Where the ruined walls of the palace give shelter to the vegetation it grows in tropical luxuriance. I judged the Pampas grass to be twelve feet, and the Chusan palms fourteen feet in height. There is an avenue of Ilex,

LAMPHEY PALACE

and time has wreathed the mouldering walls with many a curious climber, where soon I found a robin's nest.

Our visit to Lamphey is very hurried; and we are sorely puzzled whether to go to Carew or to Manorbere on our homeward way to Tenby. We are told Carey (as they call it) is about a mile down the first turn to the left and much easier to find ; so, off we rush to find that first turn is fully two miles distant and we are very tired.

Carew Castle is magnificent. It is a Castle for pomp and pageantry, masque, and revelry, with banqueting hall, fire-places, and enormous windows. Its history seems mainly to be of the "princelie fete" in honour of Henry VII. by Sir Rhys ap Thomas. Its situation is grand on projecting inlets of the great haven of Milford, and there is much to photograph, but our films were exhausted (all but one), and at the Castle entrance is a wondrous cross. Must we take the Castle or the cross? We had that day seen castles by the score from far Dryslwyn above the rushing Towy, at every few miles a castle, mostly in ruins, at Carmarthen a gaol ; but here is a cross older by centuries than any of them and miraculously preserved to-day. It stands erect on a mound by the roadside very difficult to photograph, and it appears to be almost new, but the writing on it is in a forgotten hand—prehistoric—no one knows, but some one guesses the inscription to be "The cross of the son of Ilteut the son of Ecett." The memory of them is forgotten, and possibly has been forgotten for a thousand years. We took the cross.

Then came a weary journey to Tenby, for the long May day had faded and we had to cross a lonely common where the tracks were mixed, and we went slightly astray, but we found our hotel in safety, had it all to ourselves, and, as I looked from my bedroom window, a fleet of red-sailed fishing-boats was sailing round the bay of Tenby in the glorious moonlight within a few yards it seemed of where I slept, and a more lovely and peaceful scene it would be hard to conceive.

The goal of our pilgrimage was won and further travels were uncertain, for, although the weather had been fair and good for travelling since we left Brecon, it had been cold and grey, but I wished to push on to St. Davids, and had made all needful inquiries for the journey. X was very dubious about his photo-

CAREW CROSS

graphs, as we carried films for lightness, but at last he consented to go on, and we took the train to Pembroke Dock, ferried over Milford Haven, where the seagulls sat on the buoys and the butter and bacon boats from Ireland caused a stir among the natives, took the train again for Haverfordwest, and there had seven hours for the journey over the many hills to St. Davids and back to catch another roundabout train to Tenby.

For fellow-travellers to Haverford we had a parson who, hot and hurried, nearly missed the train and gasped for breath, also a big fine young man in the Salvation Army who ought to have been a police constable. He had a mouth that would have held a whole muffin comfortably, but the respect with which he gave up his seat by the window to the one in the Apostolical Succession was noteworthy; and, though he deferentially tried to talk, it was evident that he was merely tolerated in Christian charity as a fine beetle.

We had not cycled up and down many of the hills beyond Haverford before we felt we were in a new country. The day became brilliant; the breeze from the sea; the air redolent with gorse that blazed over miles and acres; the plowed fields were purple; the whole country seemed to glow like the cohorts of Sennacherib in purple and gold, but progress was slow, and it was soon evident we should be short of time.

The sixteen miles and seventeen hills to St. Davids took us nearly three hours to travel, for we had often to walk over bad roads or steep gradients. Knowing that the return journey would take quite as long, we had only an hour left for the seeing and photographing of St. Davids. It was desperate hard work, but shall not be further mentioned, for we came again on special pilgrimage all the way from home, being on this day too hurried and tired to photograph properly or even to enjoy the never-to be-forgotten scene and country.

We did catch the return train at Ha'fordwest

and landed again at our comfortable quarters at Tenby after dark. The morrow proved wet and windy; we waited a while, went down to the shore in the wet, and round about the old Castle of Tynbye, struggled against the wind towards Caldy Island, which X said some one had been trying to sell to him; but, though he thought Tenby was the nicest seaside town he knew and its bay strongly reminded him of the famous bay of Naples, we gathered a few shells and then fled for the long journey homeward.

THE ROAD PAST PEMBROKE CASTLE

OUR SECOND PILGRIMAGE TO ST. DAVIDS

AS two pilgrimages to St. Davids count as much as one to Rome, I was not very sorry when, a few days after our return from South Wales, X told me his photographs of St. Davids were so irregular we should have to make another special pilgrimage to that rocky sanctuary, and as penance for our sins lug heavy glass-plates with us instead of films for photographing, and take our time, not fretting nor hurrying over the work, however the winds or the heathen might rage against us; for the stones that had stood the tempests and been polished by the bare feet of pilgrims for a thousand years would still be there heedless of our fussy hurry.

If any Thomas a Didymus should doubt the time-honoured fact that two pilgrimages to St. Davids are as good for him and his soul as one pilgrimage to Rome, let him journey forth to find that lonely shrine on Britain's outermost rock-fanged, storm-swept shore, feel its fascination for himself, and, if not content, he can have the authority in Latin, more or less transcribed from an indulgence of Pope Calixtus:

> "Meneviam pete bis. Romam adire si vis,
> Æqua mercestibi redditur hic et ibi:
> Roma semel quantum dat bis Menevia tantum."

> "Seek St. Davids twice. If you wish to go to Rome,
> Equal benefits are given to you here and there:
> Twice to St. Davids gives as much as once to Rome."

THE PILGRIM'S WAY

'Twas on a fine May morning I left my home at eight o'clock on heavily-laden bicycle to meet with X by the way and be whirled towards the south by the oft used train. The time is mentioned particularly, for, with the quickest travelling, we were thirteen hours on the journey, and twice that time would nearly take us to Rome.

At express speed we rush to Craven Arms, then

THE CATHEDRAL

turn to the west and gradually mount the hills of Wales. Unfortunately we find the weather here is wet and windy, but the country is lovely in its fresh garb of green, though the leaves on the trees are no more forward than they are at home. Steadily the train mounts upwards, leaving the watershed of the Severn for the Irfon and the Wye: still it goes up, amid the clouds, into a tunnel, and then we face towards the fair vale of Towy, through whose rich and varied scenery we glide for fifty miles.

Ever changing, yet ever beautiful, have been the scenes through the rich lands of Salop with the white-faced Herefords, on to the russet hills where the hardy black Welsh men and cattle live. Here are new towns called "Wells," high up in the pure air, where fat and idle hypochondriacs come to gossip and to drink, fretting their lives and their livers away in trying to recover the health they ought never to have lost. Our impatience of them is mutual, but, at Llandilo, "All change."

Here we have to wait about an hour and the rain is thick and heavy. It is not many days since we were in the town, so we stay in shelter. Our outward train is in a siding, the most picturesque or pleasantest railway siding I was ever in. Far below us the swollen river rushes on its course through fields and woods and hills. We can hear the larks sing and the cuckoo call, and feel a fresh air as we quietly sit in the train waiting and wondering how long the rain will last.

At Carmarthen we have to change carriages and wait again. Here there is a refreshment room and the weather looks better, though we almost decide to stay the night at Haverfordwest and go on to St. Davids in the morning.

The clock strikes six as we alight from the train at Haverford, and the rain has ceased. We decide to struggle on. Between us and St. Davids there are sixteen miles and seventeen hills, or thereabouts, for there is nothing the Welsh are so liberal with as their miles and their hills. There should be three hours of daylight and only one end to the road—if we keep out of the sea. The road is bad, the wind is dead against us, and we are heavily laden; but we are tired of the train, fully conscious of the arduous journey in front of us, and resolved to lose no time, but to take every possible care and precaution.

Recording time and distance by watch and cyclo-

THE CATHEDRAL

meter, I find in the first hour, that is by seven o'clock, we have done five miles and five hills. This may seem slow, but we are satisfied, for on to Keeston hill the rise has been three hundred feet and the road is drying rapidly. Further on we are suddenly engulfed in one of the grandest and most awful scenes it has ever been my lot to witness.

We go down a road shaped and graded like an upright corkscrew, covered with loose stones and apparently ending in the sea. The roar of the breakers on the rocks becomes deafening. The spray drenches us; X disappears in the mist. With both brakes jammed hard on, the bike bumps onward and downward amid the stones. Every nerve is on the stretch as one scans every yard, ready to jump off at any moment. We seem to be plunging headlong into the boiling surf and certain death. If we had not been on the road a few days before we should certainly not have ventured any further. We get safely to the bottom, behind a barrier of big pebbles and rocks, but if that barrier broke, all behind it would instantly have sudden death. We cannot hear our own voices. We are half drowned with the driven spray. Intense excitement urges us on for the quarter mile of low road, and then, like shipwrecked mariners, we thank God for life and look around in astonishment.

We have passed the sands and submerged trees and homes of old Niwegal, the inmost part of the bay of St. Bride; the tide is at its height, driven inland by the storm and gale from the Atlantic. In the waning light of evening we could see the whole semi-circle or horse-shoe of jagged rocks from Skomar's Isle to Ramsey's Isle lit up with the columns of spray that were shot from sea to sky all along those sharp-toothed cliffs. The roar of the waves was awful; the wind tossed the waters on the rocks in foam, as in a tempest; we tried to speak, but shuddered and went on.

ST. DAVIDS, CARN LLYDY IN DISTANCE

Two or three hundred feet almost straight up, down again, up again. Eight o'clock found us with eleven miles safely traversed in two hours, and a successful journey almost ensured. Even as we looked around and made our reckoning, the sun burst out for the first time to our great encouragement.

It had long since set at Greenwich, and our watches were set by Greenwich time; but this sun cared nought for Greenwich, and, like Joshua's at Gibeon, it hasted not to go down as we restless hurried on. For many hours we had been going west with all speed, and were well pleased the sun should show itself over the stormy sea or the mountains of Ireland when the almanacs said it had set. The dark clouds were lit up with lurid red or fiery gleams as we plunged downhill again to the sheltered harbour of Solva, where all was dark and the waters were not the seething cauldron of St. Brides.

About a score of times we had to push our bikes uphill, and, being sheltered from the wind, we were hot. Then, on the high ground, the keen and lazy wind went through us. We were wet with perspiration as we toiled upwards, but dried and chilled as we rushed down again with the wind for a brake. The spray of the sea at Newgale had been a bath; and the whole journey was rather rough for two old men, but it was a pilgrimage to be remembered as long as life lasts—a genuine pilgrimage, where rest came at length although the way was long and weary.

I think we were too much elated to feel weary when we reached our haven and hostel. We wanted supper. Our appetites were sharpened by the sea air. Our stomachs were not weakened by strong drink, nor by tobacco. We had plenty of fat bacon and eggs, with rich new milk to drink; and we went to bed to sleep the sleep of innocence while the raindrops beat on the rattling windows of the bedrooms,

THE CROSS, ST. DAVIDS

The top of the cathedral tower is shown beyond the steps to the cross.

and our lullaby was the distant roar of the breakers on the rocks, the fitful wail of wandering seabird, and the sea winds' moan.

This city of David is a wonderful place. It is not set on a hill, for the top of the tower is about on a level with the market-place. There may not be a market, for the whole population would barely be that of a good-sized hotel. It lives as it ever has

THE GATEHOUSE

lived—on its pilgrims. Its life and interest centre in its cathedral and its history. Let us shortly glance at the latter first.

David, the patron saint of Wales, whose name is vulgarly pronounced Taffy, flourished about fourteen hundred years ago. His historians say he was the product of a rape on a nun, which is not a good beginning, but it was not his fault. He was "comelye faiere, beautifull, and foure cubitts high." He preached so eloquently that the ground rose under his feet like a spring-board at a pantomime, and lifted him above his audience. When he was a young man he

THE CATHEDRAL

was told to look at some pretty girls who were bathing naked, but he promptly looked the other way, and after that his success was assured. This is a very nice miracle, and might be tried again as a test for other saints. He became archbishop, and moved the episcopate from Caerleon to Mynyw or Menevia, to get as far as ever he could from the heathen English. And it is wonderful how very few of the heathen English in our time, though they now call themselves Christians, ever saw or even ever heard of the city of David. Many of them think it is somewhere in Scotland.

Although St. David escaped the English by retiring into the utter desolation of Penbroch (the head of foam) and ruled independently of Rome or Canterbury, his home or temple was near the sea, where pagan Norsemen came, and its annals often record "Menevia vastatur."

There were twenty-five archbishops after David, and then, because of some disease, the pall was transferred to Armorica, and St. Davids became a bishopric. There were then nineteen bishops to the time when Giraldus wrote in 1188, and I wish he had written less about bishops and miracles and more about natural history.

One of the holy bishops ate flesh meat, so a band of pirates carried him off and he sent back his epitaph to the faithful who were left:

"Because I ate meat I am made meat."

The holy well, near to which the first church was probably built, flowed with wine or milk in the good old days, but we cannot test it now, for when Sir Gilbert Scott did some restorations to the cathedral he had the well turned into a drain—"restored" into the state it may have been before Noah's flood.

All sorts and conditions of men, from our greatest

THE SHRINE OF ST. DAVID

kings to our many barfoot beggars, have trodden the hard and stony paths to St. David's shrine. William the great Conqueror, who is probably the ancestor of all living Englishmen; Henry II., who puzzled with Llechllavar, the talking stone, jumped it unscathed; Edward Longshanks, not content with his pilgrimage to Palestine and his many perilous wanderings over land and sea, with countless others struggled here, that here

TOMBS OF
RHYS GRYG   ST. DAVID

in this stormy solitude their orisons might bring them the desire of their hearts.

The bones of David were carried to battle to bring victory from the Lord, and they may have been lost by the way; but, in the ages of faith, they brought gifts and money in heaps, until the monks were said to divide them every week in dishfuls. The offerings were put in the quatrefoil openings of the tomb and from thence went down spouts into locked coffers.

It would be vain for me to attempt to give any

description of the cathedral. The pictures show its beauties far better than I could, but they cannot convey the sense of quietude and remoteness that so appealed to us. We never saw one pilgrim or worshipper or any one but the verger the morning we were there. It is only the third time we have ever spent some hours photographing in a church. The beautiful pictures of Tong and of Tewksbury were the products of the former work.

A WINDOW IN THE CATHEDRAL

Our early morning at St. Davids boded ill, for all was misty and gloomy. The first business with X at any new place is the sending off of postcards. He buys them in dozens and scribbles them off to any one he can think of. The difficulty here is to find any. The city of David is not a city of shops, and the people are not many. The children do not know the meaning of the words "stationers," "postcards." At what appears to be a chemist's they sell pills, papers, perfumes, postcards, photographs, &c. I suggest we go to the cathedral at once, out of the damp, and take our own photographs while we pray for better weather. The postcards must be sent whether the weather is better or worse.

There is a short cut down the hill to the cathedral of thirty-nine steps, and when X hears these steps are called the "Thirty-Nine Articles," he impiously declares he doesn't believe the Articles and won't go down the steps. He sluthers along down the wet grass and rocks at dangerous risk to the precious camera and plates. Then, inside the cathedral, he tries to adjust the machine to take the nave, but is a long time about it, and becomes so impatient I ask him what is the matter. He says he cannot get it level;

everything is askew; and he hopes I shall not remind him of the Thirty-Nine Articles. I tell him he is too particular; I had to swallow the Thirty-Nine Articles whether I liked them or not, having "to bring my mind to things, if things were not to my mind": and if he means to photograph this splendid old church he will have to reconcile himself to the fact

THE PARLOUR

GOWER'S TOMB

that its floor is not level, nor nearly level, for it goes up a steep gradient, and its main pillars are not upright, neither do its arches appear to correspond. Nevertheless it is one of the most beautiful churches I have seen, its interior being far better than its exterior. Outside it is in almost constant storm; inside the stones are mellowed purple, warmly tinted.

Our devotions in the cathedral being over, there are the beautiful ruins all around to see. But X objects at once to the bishop's palace. What is the good of a bishop? What right has he to a palace? The happy thought comes to me to mildly explain that this bishop's palace is in ruins. "So it ought to be," he answers. "Well, then, let us show the ruin that has rightly fallen on the magnificent home of the successors of the Apostles, men who had not where to lay their heads." That pacifies him, he makes a few exposures and leaves me amid the crumbling ruins to meditate in peace.

Peace! Where can peace be found? It is not here, even in the desolation of this once magnificent palace. Every coign of vantage has its jackdaw—chattering, squabbling, scolding. Every one is dressed in shiny black with a fringe of grey round the back of the head as if it were some survival of the tonsure. Are the spirits of former tenants in them, and is this a May meeting of the clergy? Listen to the hoarse croaker who keeps his daw-eye on us as he perches over the chief seat in the banqueting hall. "Dearly beloved, we haunt the holy places, for ours still they are. Here we chatter and preach and pray, for our Heavenly Father feedeth us. We take the fruit from neighbours' gardens; we suck our neighbours' eggs; we devour the widows' chickens; and, for a pretence, we make long prayers." "Ha, ha, ha, ha—a!" rings out from far on high, the wild mocking laugh of the Kittiwake gull. Ha, ha, ha! What is it this wanderer says? Does

THE BISHOP'S PALACE

he mock at men who plod this stony earth to earn their daily bread. The joy of living makes him careless of the morrow—take no thought for the morrow. In

IN THE BISHOP'S PALACE

the bright light of heaven are countless seabirds floating, wheeling, gliding by, all laughing as they fly. Four feet of snowy wings bears past a herring gull, whose throat gurgles and whose golden bill shakes as he looks down on poor me and in derision laughs his weird laugh. "On tireless wings we float in air, the sea gives us our food, we want no better and we wish for nothing new; why cannot man be content?" Ha, ha, ha! comes fainter from afar, and the sea winds' moan brings back the echo, Ha, ha, ha!

I wonder how it is that jackdaws, the greatest thieves of all birds, and their relations the rooks, inhabit churches or their neighbourhood, while in commercial cities like Manchester the pigeon or dove, the bird of peace and love, makes its home. Of course if the jackdaws came they would soon swallow all the eggs and young of the pigeons, if they could find them. At St. Davids, as at Wells, the jackdaws swarmed, and consequently other birds were scarce. I saw an empty cartridge in the grass, so I was comforted with the thought that sometimes the sinner would be cut off and the hypocrite's hope perish.

Giraldus Cambrensis, whose tomb and dust are still in the cathedral, mentions these black rogues in his day, saying they were quite tame to any one who was dressed in black. If they have been breeding in and in ever since they are not likely to improve.

The history by Giraldus of his travels through Wales as he sought recruits for a crusade, have many bits of natural history that should be better known. The broad-tailed beavers were in the Teivi or Tyvy in his day, and he describes their curious habitations and their cunning ways. This river, whose short name is spelt in five different ways in the first five books I have consulted, was the best river for salmon. Some salmon were so strong that if they were put in a coracle and struck the side with their tail they overset the boat. He mentions the golden-plumaged oriole whistling to them when they were too exhausted to whistle. The oriole is now extinct and the kite is very rare. A few kites still nest in mid-Wales, but every year the insatiable egg collectors manage to rob the nests, and

THE BISHOP'S PALACE

soon they will be no more. King Henry II., waiting to sail to Ireland, was flying a Norwegian hawk (possibly a gyr falcon) in Pembroke when a wild peregrine dropt from the sky and struck it dead at the King's feet. After that the King would have his peregrines from St. Davids Head or the Isle of Ramsey, where some of these grand birds vainly try to rear their young even now.

Probably the first mention of Cheshire's famous cheese is by Giraldus, for they brought him cheese made from the milk of deer when he went to Chester. There were no nightingales, for his archbishop said they followed wise counsel and never came into Wales. An eagle on Snowdon wore away a stone by sharpening its beak on it on every fifth holiday. It apparently expected carnage after holidays.

The result of this preaching of the crusade through Wales was—three thousand of the best fighting men, all skilled in war, armed and impatient to fight, took the cross, called themselves Christians, and set out to slay. It reminds me of an answer I lately heard from a missionary. There were some differences between a missionary and his employers. The chairman of the magistrates asked him, "What was the first and chief duty of a missionary?" the ready answer came, "To collect subscriptions."

One great man in Wales was willing to take the cross, but was asked, "Are you not going to consult your wife?" With downcast look he modestly answered, "When the work of a man is to be undertaken the counsel of a woman ought not to be asked." What a priestly answer! Of course he was given the cross, but did the wife catch him?

Here is Giraldus's description of St. Davids, written more than seven hundred years ago: "Menevia is in a most remote corner on the Irish Sea. Its soil is stony, sterile, barren, neither clothed with woods, nor distinguished with rivers, nor adorned with meadows, always exposed to winds and tempests, constantly open to attacks by—." Excepting the last few words, the description is a good one to-day. X rejoices in this remote and primitive country; he says it is bracing and open, and reminds him of Derbyshire. It certainly is much better than Derbyshire, with Stockport, Sheffield, and Chesterfield at its corners, coal-pits and lime-kilns up and down. A later traveller described the little city as a wretched village, where misery and

WINDOW OF THE BISHOP'S BANQUETING HALL

beggary stared him in the face. It is generally supposed you can get nothing to eat or drink there. We fared sumptuously every day. We saw the cows, whose milk was good, and the hens that laid eggs where the jackdaws could not get them. There were sheep also and pigs; but the flour would have to come from a drier clime. The chief food of the natives used to be seabirds; but, as we were there in the nesting season, we refrained from asking for any.

Owen of Henllys, writing in 1603, says: "The plentie of fowles was incredible. The baser sort of labouringe men had fyve meales a daye in their season, for on some landes you can hardlie walke without treading on Egges in nestes. The fowles are ripe about mydsomer when they are flushe, being readye to forsake their nestes. They are very dayntie meate. Some will be taken and fedd and kept as a readye dishe all the yeare. Puffines are reputed to be fishe for those who are ceremoniouse to refrayne from fleshe at seasons.

"The mountains foster the grouse and heathcocke which are alwaies in season (!) . . . In the bogges breedeth the crane, and byttur . . . on highe trees the heronshewes, the shovler (spoonbill). . . . There are wild geese and wilde swannes, but of all fowles the chiefest are the gull and the woodcocke.

"The woodcocke althoughe he be not our countryeman borne yet wee must needes thinke him to be of some affinitie to manie of our countrie people by reason of the love and kindenes he sheweth in resortinge hither . . . for the people of this countrey are of more playne meaninge, simple, harmelesse, and farthest from Machiavill devises, or pryeing spyryttes; this fowle being noted likewise for his symplicitie . . . he cometh to the people neerest to his innocent, playne, and symple humor. . . . Yf anie Easterly winde be alofte wee shal be sure to have him before Michaelmas, for plentie yt is allmost incredible. In cockeshoote tyme, which is twylight . . . yt is no strange thinge to take a hundred or sixe score in one woodd . . . In St Dauids ij woodcockes, iij snipes, and certayne teales and black byrdes were bought for a peny . . . such penyworthes are hadd of fowles in this countrey."

Good old Owen, Lord of Kemes, he scrupled not to take the simple woodcocks in when they trusted to his "harmelesse" nature. Here followeth a copy of his handwriting from the beginning of his book: if he had "fyve" meals a day of gulls and woodcocks it is wonderfully well written.

In another part of his writings, Owen says of the Anglo-Flemish in the Englishrye about him: "Though they have not that excesse in drinkinge with which their kinsmen the Dutchmen are taxd, these our ffleminges have altered their stomackes . . . and will haue fyve meales a daie, and if you will bestowe the sixt on them they will accept of it verye kindlye, and will bestowe laboure on the seaventhe meale."

In his day, in the brook between the cathedral and "the Bushopps pallace, St. Davids trowtes for biggness exceeded any and for tamnes against nature, were not a feard at the sight of men lookinge on them, approachinge to mens handes for foode." That was in the ages of faith. Nowadays men would tempt them, deceive them, lie unto them, and eat them, therefore trout are scarce and wary; while the black thieves of jackdaws that are good for nothing still prosper in the holy places.

Woodcocks are not so plentiful in these degenerate days, for our host of the hostel considers twenty-seven as a good day's bag—he and a party from

THE COLLEGE

Lord Tredegar's having shot that number on one day of the preceding winter. One hundred were recorded in *The Field* as having been shot in three days this last Christmas. Bitterns are often killed, a pair of fine ones stuffed being in the hall of the hotel. It is a pity they cannot be left alone in peace, for what damage can they possibly do to any one more than the mild fright of their weird and distant booming.

THE PILGRIM'S WAY

In most of the inns in South Wales I notice there are stuffed otters. They seem likely to go the way of the beaver, the wild cattle, the red deer, the eagle, the kite, the quail, the crane, the spoonbill, and last, but not least, the wild-goose.

St. David forbade all noxious reptiles to come near to his holy place, for the neighbouring country is all

THE PILGRIM'S WAY

pilgrims' land and sanctuary; but what it was or is a sanctuary for I cannot quite make out. There is no specification of what St. David meant by noxious; hitherto his holy city has escaped many of the disagreeables of civilisation. We never saw, heard, smelt, felt, or tasted a motor vehicle or a steam-engine of any sort on either of our pilgrimages; but even this record of our quiet enjoyment in the month of May 1906 may cause the quiet enjoyment of others to be spoilt in the future.

Our gloomy morning had brightened into a splendid noon, and, after a stroll towards the sea, we decided to begin the homeward journey, photographing some of the many wonderfully picturesque bits on our pilgrims' way, hasting not nor resting, as we had seven hours for the seventeen hills between us and Haverfordwest and dark.

THE PILGRIM'S WAY

It is as well to state here that the photographs are very disappointing in not giving any idea of the beauties of these wild uplands on a fine day in the spring-tide, where the brilliant blue of the sky in the pure sea air, the purplish patches of plowed land, but above all the blazing glory of the golden gorse that no "topaz of Ethiopia" could equal, miles in length and miles in breadth, were all of such dazzling brightness that we seemed to be nearer to heaven, wandering for one brief day in the havens of the blessed.

The pictures also fail to convey any sense of space or distance. We could often see telegraph posts apparently half a mile or so distant, but between us and them there was a great gulf fixed down part of which we might rush at the breakneck speed of twenty miles an hour, but up which we had to laboriously climb at two miles an hour.

THE PILGRIM'S WAY

The scent of the gorse was as powerful as the scent of clover or of beans in flower. X would not believe me that its brilliant colour would only be black in the photograph; but I had tried yellow azaleas with purple rhododendrons in flower, and found the former developed black and the latter white.

Very reluctantly we turned our backs on the picturesque peaks of Carn Llydy and Penbyry, the distant headland of St. Davids, and the tiny city with its venerable shrine. Rocks in the sea are called the

ST. BRIDE'S BAY
Nineteen hours after the high-tide and storm

"bishop and his clerks," and, as there is always some one to criticise the clergy, it was long since said of them that if they do preach deadly doctrine they do keep residence, *i.e.* they are not always in England. Their best qualities are they "yelde good store of gulls in tyme of yeare," whereas most clergy would use the gulls for themselves.

Other rocks have the more vulgar name of "bitch and pups"; they may cause more noise than the others, for a furious current rushes past them, and all this stormy, rock-fanged, holy coast, even the bay of St. Bride, is safest and best when seen from the land.

Our homeward journey was far easier than the toilsome struggle of the previous evening, and nowhere was the difference more marked than at the sands of Newgale, where the storm of wind and spray was so fearful before. The tide was out and the gentle waves were glistening in the sun. We stopped at the little inn and coaxed the old lady into letting us have tea. While that was being prepared, we climbed the bank of shingle, and, "by the sad sea waves," we gathered cockspur shells as in the days of yore. We might have been two Robinson Crusoes with no other man within miles —an almost boundless expanse of sea and sand and rocks around. How that old woman can live alone with one girl to help is strange; but she is used to it. Years ago she here kept an inn or house of call, was busy enough on fine Sundays in the summer, but lonely for months of winter. It is said she prospered and saved money, but on a stormy night the floods arose and beat upon her house, and it fell. She had heard of Noah, and though she had no ark ready, she had a big tub for the brewing of ale, and she got into that and floated safely up the little valley on to a miniature

Ararat, from whence she was rescued in the morning. It is believed she saved her money and her ducks, but not her pigs. Another house was built, and there we tried to talk, but she would not be communicative. The tea that had been so much trouble to boil, was charged at the rate of sixpence each, so we

THE PILGRIM'S WAY
A very lonely home.

paid her and the girl also, and then learnt that the Duke of Cambridge had been there, and when he told her he was married, she asked him what he had done with his wife. Why was not the missus with him?

Our little pilgrim-band went joyfully on its homeward way. There was no fear of missing the road, for there was only one road. We could see for miles where white-washed farmsteads dotted the purple patches that were set in frames of gold, but the ways to them seemed to be merely tracks across the fields. Here and there were walls of stone, with an upright cromlech (or what looked like one) in the middle of a field, for the cattle to rub against. There were great hedges of gorse, and there were hobbled sheep. Primroses and violets grew by the roadside where they could. No artist who ever lived could do justice to one picture that we saw—a very large field on a hillside; a plowman slowly plodding up long furrows in the purple earth; every furrow changing colour as the sunlight or the shadows pass across; the furrows of yesterday faded and paler than those of to-day; even the morning's lighter than the evening's; and over all were myriads of seagulls—screaming, sweeping, whirling round, as they closely followed the plow heedless of the man, as if they thought his work was for them and they were helping him—

"Far below, the vast and sullen swell
Of ocean's Alpine azure rose and fell."

A few more hills with steep ravines and we say good-bye to the sea. We had been down to it at the little harbour or creek of Solva, and again at Newgale; now there are hills before us for endless miles, and a lonely peel-tower is seen from afar. It is the lofty Norman castle or watch-tower of Roch, still standing dominant over all the land for miles, typical of the Norman power. It was the furthest outpost of the Englishry, the little England beyond Wales, known as Southern Pembrokeshire. St. Davids and all our route down the vale of Towy were Welsh of very Welsh, but Pembroke and Haverfordwest were the strongholds of the Anglo-Fleming settlement, whose progeny to

ROCH CASTLE

this day have not amalgamated with the Ancient Britons.

Roch Castle has been "restored"; in fact the "restoration" is still going on. It makes one sad to see those modern windows in the stern old walls, but the modern inmates may be delicate, and the visitors may not like fresh air even in the summer. It was difficult to photograph, and not picturesque when it was taken, its beauty (if it has any) being in its lofty, lonely height.

The long day's work was done, and the daylight far spent when we safely arrived at civilisation again. The coffee-room of a stuffy town hotel, with nigger minstrels outside, was very uncongenial after our previous night's rest, where the only sounds were of the storm of wind and rain, the moaning of the sea, and the seabird's wail.

It was fortunate we had made the return journey over the wild country on a fine evening, for the next morning dawned with steady, persistent rain, so we took the first express train and fled.

We had the train to ourselves, or nearly so, as far as Carmarthen or Llandilo, where we were joined by a man who, I felt certain, was an official or legal adviser to some public body in the north. He bought *The Daily Liar*, read it all the way, and took no notice of anything else. When we moved to his window to see Dryslwyn Castle on its height with the swollen river foaming round it, he did glance at it, but his eyes reverted at once to read of tonics and pills.

Further on the bored dyspeptics from the Wells crowded in, and we had to suffer them and their jargon as best we could. There was no chance of breaking the journey, for the weather seemed to be settled wet, so we were thankful to get safely home. The first and third days had been incessantly wet, and we had

HOME AGAIN 175

been incessantly travelling by train, but the second or principal day was fine, worth all the trouble and expense of our glorious second pilgrimage to the city and shrine of St. David.

ROCH CASTLE

CONWY—PLAS MAWR—GWYDYR—DOL-WYDDELAN—HARLECH—CORS Y GEDOL—CYMMER—HENGWRT—LLANEGRYN—DOLAU GWYN

AS our pilgrims' ways had taken us right across South Wales from east to west, so we now ventured in like manner to cross the heart of Cambria, leaving the mountains of Snowdon on our right as we journeyed from the well-known Castle of Conwy, up old Conwy's foaming flood, to the lonely castled crag in the wilderness where the great Llewelyn first felt the keen air of his native hills, and over mountains of slate to that other stately ruin still standing erect above the Irish Sea, and known by name o'er all the world from the music of the march of its men.

In dull and heavy weather we travelled by train from Cheadle, and, after many changes through Warrington and Chester, we safely came to Conwy where all was serene and bright. I am spelling the name of the famous little town as it was spelt in 1185 in the charter of Llewelyn, and as Pennant spelt it in 1781, the old-fashioned picturesque way, for why should a superfluous and misleading letter be inserted, when the old is better. I am also refraining from attempting to write much of the history or to give any description of the place, for most of our countrymen know something of it already, and the young ladies who wonder why the Castle was built so near to the railway station may be content with looking at the pictures.

To roll on a bicycle along a good road on a suspen-

CONWY

sion bridge over a rushing tide, and then to be pulled up at a castellated gateway with a demand for your money or your life—that is, pay or you will be knocked off your bicycle—seems rather a jumble of styles and times. There is also some difficulty about return fares

IN PLAS MAWR

—some curious calculations that I forget—but we get off by paying, as one gets off most things by paying, and we go first to Plas Mawr, where we find the curator whom I had known years ago, and with him we spend an hour or so (that being all we could spare) in photographing this old home of the Wynnes.

As the world artistic knows, Plas Mawr is tenanted

THE FIREPLACE IN THE BANQUETING HALL

by the Royal Cambrian Academy of Art, and the numerous pictures which adorn its walls, having white mounts and glass fronts, are very bothering to photographers. The old house is well kept and well cared for, the contemporary furniture being good. The use now made of it is the best use it can have, and I wish every old town in the kingdom that has a fine old house in it—and there are many—would maintain it and learn of Plas Mawr and of Hall i' th' Wood.

Perhaps the chief feature of this "Great Place" is the decorative plaster-work of the ceilings and mantelpieces; the amount of animals, coats of arms, dates, initials, &c. done in plaster all over the place is very great, and the patterns or designs of the ceilings all differ from one another. In the picture of the mantelpiece in the banqueting hall, any one with good eyesight may see the initials R. W. halfway up the outside figures and the shield of arms of Robert Wynne in the centre, with the figures 15-80 for the date on either side of the shield. On the extreme right there is shown a bit of the massive banqueting table that has long outlasted those who used to feast at it, and is not yet worn out. The floor is rather worn, for it has become billowy or rolling, giving one the delightful feeling of having dined without any of the consequences thereof.

Adjoining the banqueting-hall is the necessary kitchen, with its great arched fireplace, where we are shown the stone worn away by the sharpening of knives. There seems to have been a deal of sharpening, but in those days men ate Billy-goats, and their sinews would soon blunt any knife. A bit of hung-goat dried up the chimney would be something like a log of aromatic pine. It may not all be digested even yet. I have tasted some of the famous Welsh mutton that was rather rammy, although Mr. Jones would assure you it was beautiful and charge accordingly. When we nearly killed a sheep on our pilgrimage

THE KITCHEN

IN PLAS MAWR

IN PLAS MAWR

to the World's End, our ostler told us its value was fifteen shillings, but if the farmer had seen us its value would be £5.

There is a good old stone oven for the baking of bread and an old-fashioned bread-safe hanging from the ceiling. When bread was baked only once a week, or possibly once a month, it had to be kept in an open cupboard or receptacle where it would not go mouldy, and it was much safer to put it out of the reach of the feudal retainers who might gorge on feast days or when a sheep died, but who often had to fast.

As I was carefully looking up the chimney Mr. Furness, the curator, guessed I was searching for hiding-holes, and he was delighted to tell me all about them. The end of a passage can be seen high up inside the chimney, but no one living has ever explored it. There is a secret room by the side of the chimney and over the doorway into the kitchen. Up in the attic, where we had to walk very delicately over the rafters, we were shown a trap-door, giving access to a cell from whence an inner secret chamber could be entered. These hidden holes for fugitives are very interesting, but, unfortunately, there are no records or even legends to tell us how the priest escaped, or the beautiful young Cavalier in the blue silk stockings and the golden hair was concealed by the charming daughter of the horrid Puritan, while the crop-eared Roundheads snuffled psalms in their noses until they got very drunk and the handsome captain of the Cavaliers went for his trusty men to punish the scurvy rogues.

The lack of history and the high ideals of the Royal Cambrian Academy of Art have caused rooms in Plas Mawr to be described as Queen Elizabeth's, though there is nothing to show she was ever in them; her arms and initials having doubtless been placed in them by her Celtic kindred, who knew the only way to get anything from her was by flattery. What is called her room

THE WYNNE ROOM

was probably the private parlour of the Wynnes. There are other initials and arms on the walls. R. W. stands for Robert Wynne; D. G. for Dorothy Griffith, who became Dorothy Wynne; the date 1577 is divided by a window, and there is a strange letter like a G

A CORNER OF THE COURTYARD

reversed, which the curator tells me is J, but I think it is another form of D. In R. G. they read Robert of Gwydyr, and E. R. may stand for Edwardus Rex. The bloody Saxons' heads that grin at you from among the fearful wildfowl on the walls and ceiling must make the house a creepy one to live in.

One hundred and twenty odd years ago Pennant wrote, "A more beautiful fortress never arose" than

CONWAY

this Castle "of matchless magnificence," built by the great Edward at Conwy—one of the most blood-stained, picturesque spots in Britain, or it may be even in the world. It seems to treat the railway trains that fuss around it with silent contempt. The winds soon blow their dust and smoke away. The river rushes past it for hours, and then the incoming tide rushes all the water back again until it laves the time-worn, water-worn walls. Four times a day has salt water or fresh ebbed or flowed around it for more than six hundred years, and the Castle still looks calmly on though seas may rage and storms may gather round the encircling hills. Foreign ships are anchored in its shelter; tourists of all nations throng its ruined courts; all sorts and conditions of car or carriage pay toll below its gate as if its feudal barons still exacted toll, and many are the different languages and accents we may hear within the still standing walls of the quaint, little, round-towered town.

The town itself is in the shape of a Welsh harp; the walls extending from the water to the hillside; twenty-four towers, four embattled gateways, and the great Castle make up a picture worthy of the finest illuminated, mediæval manuscript of chivalry and romance. Two of the walls were continued beyond the fortress some distance into the water, ending in round towers, but the ceaseless washing of the waves has long since levelled them.

The King himself was nearly starved into surrendering his new Castle. His supplies had been seized, and only one small cask of wine remained. The water had to be mixed with honey before the men could drink it, and some of us may remember that a fair for honey is yearly held in Conwy still. Luke de Tany crossed the river at low water, with seven knights and three hundred men. The Welsh waited for the turn of the tide, fell upon the English in force, and

FROM THE BATTLEMENTS OF CONWY

killed every man except "William le Latimer, a most strenuous knight," whose charger swam through the

THE WAY INTO THE CASTLE

rushing current with its mail-clad master and saved him.

These wars were terribly cruel. Both sides seem to have remorselessly killed any of the other side that they could catch, and the unremitting slaughter told

CONWY CASTLE

on the weaker nation. Captives were tied back to back and thrown into the river. The English were "watching, fasting, freezing, praying," and then they burnt and sacked the Abbey of Aberconwy with all its contents, chronicles, and MSS. included. One wonders if they prayed and returned thanks for that crime.

There must have been mental reservations before then, for we read Prince Dafydd took oaths of fealty to Henry III., and then offered the Pope five hundred marks to absolve him from them. The Pope agreed, but the King offered more, so the Pope, like the Scot, would say, "Honesty is the best policy." Then Dafydd trusted to the arm of flesh and smote the English with their mercenary allies.

In our own Civil War, when English and Welsh had long been one nation, the Archbishop of York was Williams, who came to take care of his native place in the interest of the King, and who gave receipts to every one for their goods and chattels that were stored in the Castle or the town. But Prince Rupert had not much faith in parsons, so he turned him out, putting Sir John Owen in his stead. Then the Archbishop sulked because much of his own private property was kept from him. As the King made no redress, he tried the Parliament and General Mytton, made a treaty with them, turned his coat, and fought with the assaulting troops. The archiepiscopal preacher of peace stormed the town, and recovered the goods of himself and his friends.

As our usual fate is to hurry we had to leave Conwy long before we wished, for we were to sleep at Bettws, and to cycle up the far-famed vale where artists most do congregate. We chose the right or Aberconwy side of the river, for I knew from experience the gradients of the road are easier, and possibly the views are finer. We were lucky to have a glorious evening, with clouds and sunlight chasing one another over the great range of Snowdon's hills. The gleaming river lessens as we go up, but the cloud-capped moun-

tains come nearer; the haze is bluer, the woodlands more luxuriant though steeper, and evening's glow lights up the heather and the rocks. I regret we had not time nor plates to photograph, for soon we found Llanrwst, and hurried to the church that is so nicely hidden from the little town.

A few yards from the market-place, behind the old-fashioned houses, is a country churchyard, where yews stretch their long arms over a salmon river where men are fishing and gulls are screaming by. The chapel built against the church for " Rich Wynne

THE EMPTY COFFIN OF LLEWELYN THE GREAT

of Gwyder in 1634" by Inigo Jones, contains the monuments we wish to see, but better work by far than Jones's is the fine carved rood-screen from the ruined Abbey of Aberconwy. From the same ruin is the stone coffin of Llewelyn the Great, empty enough now; where are the bones and the dust of the patriot?

There is also an effigy of Howell Coytmor, who fought at Poictiers ages ago. I think he is not the Sir Howell y Fwyall, or Sir Howell of the battle-axe who, with his axe, chopped off the head of the French

LLANRWST BRIDGE

King's horse, and thereby took the King prisoner in that famous battle; but eyes grow dim and brains reel in trying to disentangle all the aps and Howells in the terrible pedigree of the Wynnes. By special command of the King of England, eight yeomen served a "messe of meat" daily before Sir Howell's battle-axe that had blood on its edge, as it had in the presence of the King, and the drink was blood and water.

Over the sons of John Wynne there is an enormous stone with the strange inscription, "Funus, Fumus, Fuimus, Ecce." The meaning of the puzzle may be "Death comes, Breath is a vapour, We have been, That is all."

In my boyhood's days it was the custom for travellers over Llanrwst Bridge to have it shaken for them by some one banging their back against the wall at the side. The bridge would shiver, and the girls would scream. There were always idlers ready for the job if the amateur was afraid of injuring his spine, but the custom seems to have died, or possibly the authorities have interfered.

Bettws-y-Coed is a charming place for a quiet night's rest. There are good hotels with all a town can give, but without the noise and clatter of the streets, for they are in the country where you may sleep with your window wide open and hear nothing all night but the soothing rippling of the little river or the monotonous croak of a distant crake. As day dawns the lambs may call for their mother, or the cows may welcome the milker, or there may be much twittering of the birds, but these are sounds that we of the country love to hear when we are half asleep and half awake, quiet and happy. Of the tumult of the city there is none.

The next day we devote to Gwydyr. It is generally called a castle, but seems to me to be a comfortable old manor-house, with some of the best furniture, carving, panelling, historical relics, &c. that we have ever seen in any house, all well preserved and well kept, not "restored" nor modernised, no shoddy, no shams, nor black oak. Visitors are admitted at certain times, but never to photograph; therefore we fully

THE DOORWAY, GWYDYR

appreciate the kindness of Earl Carrington in allowing us to roam about and make pictures of what we liked.

For the ancient history of the Wynne family there are the valuable records of Sir John—writings that show the deeds and thoughts of a man, not of a thing who made a book of commonplace platitudes. Interesting as they are to me, the constant repetition of names makes genealogical puzzles that are not only wearisome to the flesh, but to the spirit and eyesight also.

Gwydyr, in its many forms, is from *Gwaed-dir*, "the field of blood": a name that would do for any part of Wales. The blood that has been spilt at Conwy, or at scores of ruined castles, or on hill sides all along the blood-stained borderland by Rhuddlan, Montgomery, Clun, and Brecon round to Cardiff and Pembroke, must surely be a hundred-fold of all that has drenched the earth of Gwedir. The blame cannot all be laid on the English. When they were left alone the Welsh slaughtered one another so constantly that if they had not been wonderfully good breeders the race would have been extinct. Hearken to some of Sir John's "cursoriwise" remarks on his ancestors.

Owen Gwynnedd, Prince of Wales, had about sixteen sons recorded who were grown up men. The eldest had a broken nose, which was very likely, so they called him Yerwerth Drwndwn, or "gammy Edward," and would not let him reign, so David reigned in his stead, married the sister of King Henry the Second, and was a great man. But Yerwerth had a son, Llewelyn, who became greater, for he killed his uncle David with all his seed and breed He married Joan, one of the chance daughters of King John, and a beautiful stone coffin was made for her which became very useful for a cattle trough for generations at a farm called the Friars.

A later ancestor, Jevan ap Robert, ap Meredydd, ap Howell, ap Dafydd, ap Gryffydd, ap Cariadog, ap &c. &c. was a goodly personage, who had not only "turmoyles abroad but deadly feuds at home in his doore, a warre more dangerous than the other." His brother-in-law had bickerings with him, and many men were slayne through the stirring woman who never gave over to make debate. She got the parson

GWYDYR

murthered, but "the three murtherers were all slayne by my ancestor, who, in a rage, himself strucke off the heads of two of them. Soe bloody and irefull were quarrels in those days, and the revenge of the sword at such libertie, as almost nothing was punished by law, whatsoever happened."

"The fashion was that the gentlemen and their retainers met to shoote matches: there was noe gentlemen of worth in the countrey but had a wine-cellar of his owne, which wine was sold to his profit; thither came his friends to meet him, and there spente the day in shooting, wrestling, throwing the sledge, and other actes of activitie and drinkeing. . . . In that wild worlde every man stood upon his guard, and went not abroad but in sort and soe armed, as if he went to encountre with his enemies."

Jevan ap Robert was very tall, and his wife was sister to Howell ap Rhys, who hired a butcher to get behind Evan at one of these sports and kill him, but to mind Evan's foster-brother, Robin ap Inko, a sharp little fellow, whose eye was ever on his foster-brother. The butcher forgot Robin, who seems to have kept his other eye on him, for just as he was striking at Evan from behind, Robin felled him—and so he died.

A cousin Gruffith assaulted Howell in his own house, and burnt his barns and outhouses, but, though armed at all points, he was "shot through the sight of his beaver into the head and slayne outright." Howell was taken with a gleve in his hand and accused of murder, but both sides were afraid of being all murdered before they could get to Carnarvon Castle. Then "it fell out by law that the burning of Howell's and assaulting him in his owne house was a more haynous offence than the death of Gruffith . . . but Howell never durst come to his owne again."

In 1468 every house in Harlech, Denbigh, Llanrwst, and the vale of Conwy was burnt to "cold

CAMBRIA DESOLATE

coals"—that is, to cinders; and Sir John writes that in his day "the very stones of the ruines of manie habitations in and along my demaynes carry yet the colour of the fire." In the days of Glyndwr the country had been so badly wasted that grass grew in the streets of Llanrwst, and the wild deer fled to

GWYDYR

the churchyard as to a sanctuary. This utter desolation lasted for many years. All men seemed to have been outlawed for murder; and a lordship of the Knights Hospitallers of St. John of Jerusalem having privilege of sanctuary, was a receptacle for any thief or murderer, who could from thence ravage the country with impunity.

But, to leave these good old times for something nearer, Meredydd ap Jevan, great-grandfather to the historian, was fostered by an honest freeholder who had lands but no children: he sent his foster-child to Carnarvon to school, where he learnt English and Latin, a matter of great moment in those days. He married and bought the castle and frithes of Dolwyddelan, for in his own inheritance there was nothing but killing and fighting. "I must either kill mine

DOLWYDDELAN CHURCH

owne kinsmen or be killed by them," was his judgment of the situation. He built a new house near Dolwyddelan, but was none too quiet even on Sundays, for if he went to church he had to leave "the doores sure barred and boulted, and a watchman to stand at the Carreg y Big during divine service—a rock whence he might see both the church, and the house, and raise the crie if the house was assaulted. He durst not, although he were guarded with twenty tall archers, make knowne when he went to church

GWYDYR

or elsewhere, or goe or come the same way through the woodes and narrow places lest he should be layed for."

To strengthen himself he got "the tallest" and ablest men as tenants. For Pencraig Inko in Gwedir ten shillings and four pence was paid. In Sir John's time it was worth £30 a year. I wonder what is the value now. "Gruffith ap Tudur felled eighteen oakes in one day. Rys ap Robert was a tall stout man, who had forsaken his freehold land at Bangor as he had killed a man and had to flee." Tall and stout means big and brave. The chieftain's force gradually grew to "seven score tall bowmen arrayed in armolett coate, steele cappe, short sword and dagger, with bow and arrowes; most of them alsoe had horses and chasing staves."

The old gentleman evidently took great care of himself. He had twenty-six children, and managed to keep body and soul together until 1525. His son appears as John Wynne ap Meredith of Gwedir, who died in 1553, and the grandson of John was Sir John, the historian; but I cannot find from whence the name of Wynne came. The Tudors had come to the throne, and it became the fashion in Wales to be more like the English.

In addition to leaving us many interesting manuscripts, Sir John Wynne kept up the reputation of his beautiful country for fecundity. With one wife, Sidney Gerard, he had eleven sons, but this was far behind his neighbour, Nicolas Hoottes of Conwy, whose monument records he was the forty-first child of his father, and the father of twenty-seven children. I expect they counted daughters in this last case, although, as a rule, in those days daughters "didn't count." Some of our Manchester merchants used to keep ledger accounts for their various children, and the cost of their keep, with their names and addresses, could soon be ascertained by applying to the ledger-clerks.

It was this wonderful fecundity in the healthy climate that intensified the evils of gavelkind in a country that was fertile in places but very rocky and barren in adjoining places. Gavelkind is the custom

GWYDYR GARDEN

of tenure whereby land is inherited from a father by all the sons in equal parts, and from a brother by all the brothers in equal parts. Sir John says it is "the destruction of Wales, the subdivision of gavelkind bringing the posterity of landholders to the estate of meane freeholders, and soe having forgotten their descents and pedigree, are become as they had never been." Which may be rendered, "If you have no pedigree you may as well be dead." An aphorism worthy of my companion but not for me, whose father never left him the sixteen quarterings for the family shield.

Sir John must have had to "bridle his choller at the dam'd crew" very often. He is the authority for the legend of the massacre of the bards by Edward I., and describes them as men who, in ancient

A CEDAR AT GWYDYR

time were wont to sing and to keep pedigrees. As further showing the loss from not having pedigrees, he says, "Poverty soone forgets whence it be descended, for it is an ancient received saying that there is noe poverty but is descended of nobilitie, nor noe nobilitie but is descended of beggerie.

'When Adam delv'd and Eve span
Who was then a gentleman?'

Yet a great temporall blessing it is and a greate heart's ease to a man to find that he is well descended,

CLEMATIS. GWYDYR

and a great griefe it is for upstarts whose descents are base, for such sort hate gentlemen in their hearts, for noe other cause but that they were gentlemen."

Perhaps he refers to the Lord Chancellor Egerton, the Cheshire bastard, who founded some great families on litigation and the wrecks of the religious houses, and objected to Sir John Wynne being on the commission of the peace for the county of Carnarvonshire. But his "kindred clave like burres," and although that might be a nuisance, and although "gavelkind chops our inheritance," I find recorded on another page "the most parte of that towne of Maethebrood is in our brood, blessed be God!"

Sir John kept a tame parson in his house at Gwedir, and gave him written instructions how to govern himself. Here are some extracts from the orders: "In the morning you should rise and say prayers in my hall to my houshold below before they go to work and when they come in at nygt. . . . Before dinner you are to come up and attend grace, and to set up above the chyldren. . . . When the table from half downwards is taken up, then are you to rise and to walk in the alleys near at hand until grace time; and to come in then for that purpose. After dinner, if I be busy, you may go to bowles, shuffelbord, or other honest decent recreation. . . . Avoyd the alehouse, to sytt and keepe drunkards company ther being the greatest discredit your function can have." It was rather hard on his reverence that he had to leave the dining-room with the children when the best tales were being told, and walk about the passage, possibly for hours, while his betters were enjoying themselves, and then be ordered in again to wind up with grace and nothing more—not an odd glass in the good old days before teetotallers had been invented.

With "a noate" of some of Sir John's wardrobe I will respectfully take leave of him. "Imprimis,

OLD-FASHIONED FINERY

one tawnie klothe cloake lined thoroughe with blacke velvett . . . two ridinge coates, laced with silke and golde lace. . . . One white satten doublett and blacke satten breeches, one silke grogram suite . . . one redd quilte waskoote . . . two pare of blacke silke stockins, one pare of perle colour silke stockins . . . one russett frize jerkin . . . two pare of white boots, one pare of

FORMAL GARDEN AND YEW

russet boots, three pare of newe blacke boots . . . two pare of damaske spurres, three pare of guilte spurres." "What a toff!"

Gwydyr House or Hall (there is nothing of the castle about it) stands close to the side of the lane from Llanrwst to Bettws through the woods at the base of the steep hill known as Carreg-y-Gwalch, or the rock of the falcon. Peregrines probably nested in the crag before and after that human freebooter, Dafydd ap Shenkin, whose spurs still hang in the Gwydyr Chapel, made it his headquarters. This Dafydd ap Shenkin was kinsman to Howell ap Rhys, and helped him to try to murder Jevan ap Robert and his breed, as before related: but I must leave these family feuds, for they cannot be as interesting to us as they were to them.

No one travelling by Gwydyr could have any idea of the charming old home he was passing. Not one-tenth of the hurrying crowds would pause to cast a second glance at the shields of arms upon its stately portal. The dragons might please them, or the curly tailed lion on the top, and there are seats for the tired wanderer who may find the date 1555 and the letters I. W., the cognizance of John Wynne, ap Meredydd, ap Jevan, ap a hundred other folk.

When X and I first went on pilgrimage to many a fine old home, he used to tell me it was just the place he would like to live at, and wonder if it was on sale. Time has worn away his longings, and he says he wants for nothing now. But at Gwydyr there is a sharp return of the malady. He says a few years ago he could have bought it for an old song and would not even trouble to look at it. Now he finds it is priceless, unrestored, unspoilt, unchanged. What luck! Oh! Look at those Queen Anne chairs of walnut, and that linen-fold panelling of aged oak; it will take twenty minutes to photograph them. When I say that is all the more reason for getting on with our work or we shall be here till tea time, he sadly replies, "you never have any sympathy."

Earl Carrington had a paper on the castle printed for the British Archæological Association when they visited North Wales in 1887. From it I try to learn more about our pictures, but there appear to be some misprints. His lordship mentions the breakfast-room, containing a curious stone chimney-piece, dated 1597. That must be the room shown on page 213, where one may read, Julius 1497 Augustus and, by the

THE ENTRANCE TO GWYDYR

great shield, the motto, "Nec timet nec tumet." Let any one who has the least knowledge or care for an old home and its furniture examine this photograph to his or her heart's content. I will merely add the ceiling is covered with emblazoned coats of arms that are but faintly shown in the picture.

In the dining-room are four fine and genuine old oak tables. Note the chairs and the candelabra on the walls. The ceiling is blue, and the mantelpiece is dated 1642. There are family portraits; one, we are told, is of Peter, the nineteenth Lord Willoughby de Eresby. Whether that is "the good Lord Willoughby," and whether the lady is the Lady Barbara, I am not sure. The great feature of this room is the pillared doorway, the pillars being believed to be the work of Inigo Jones.

The Wynne records say that Inigo Jones built the chapel and the bridge at Llanrwst and something at Gwydyr. The date on the dining-room chimney-piece was in his time, and if he was not actually a native of the place as tradition says, it is likely his father was and that the father migrated to London. It is said the son was christened Ynyr, but being sent to study in Italy, he could not be confounded with such a barbarous name, and therefore it blossomed into Inigo.

The drawing-room is evidently two stories in height, with tapestry round the upper part, and it is filled with historical furniture. In the place of honour is the picture of Sir John Wynne, that has been often engraved for illustrating histories of his time. He appears as a prosperous and portly old gentleman, in tall hat and ruff, well pleased with himself and the good things around him. The portrait of his great-granddaughter, Mary Wynne, the heiress who became Duchess of Ancaster, is beside his. There is the beautiful cradle of her father, Sir Richard Wynne. It is inlaid with various woods that mark R. W. 1634.

A VERY OLD ROOM

THE DINING-ROOM.

THE DRAWING-ROOM

A small plain table in the middle of the room was made by our present Queen in her hours of ease. The big chair to the right of the fireplace was made by Peter the Great of Russia when he was learning various crafts in England. Just beyond it in our picture is a singular Gothic chair, and there are venerable and valuable chairs that were brought from Spain by the Sir Richard who accompanied Charles the First when he went there in search of a beautiful princess. Older still is a curious little screen that was daintily worked in silk by Mary Queen of Scots, and older by ages than any of them is the ancient bell of Dolwyddelan.

The ghost-room charms us. We never saw a better. It is about the size of my own bedroom, just big enough to hold a bedstead, a chest, and a chair. This bedstead is canopied, dated 1511, with flowers or twining serpents on the bed quilt, all worked by Mary Wynne. The ceiling is like the starry firmament on high, with all the blue ethereal sky. There are very old pictures, a wedding chest of 1620, big enough to hold all sorts of things, a splendid coat of arms with "Nec tumet nec timet," and a little, common, modern washing-table, quite out of character with everything else; but nowadays there are some folk who think they really must wash, although their ancestors who had the gorgeous coats of arms never washed.

There is a portrait of Ruperta the daughter of Prince Rupert and Mrs. Hughes. That seems a curious mixture, but it brought the blood-royal into the family, and blue blood is worth sacrifice.

Another portrait of Lord Oxford's "Bloudy Shoulder'd" Arabian horse shows extraordinary anatomy, with an Arab groom in attendance. The room is so small and dark that it takes a long time and clever manipulation to photograph it. But the time is not

THE GHOST ROOM

THE STATE BEDROOM

OLD SPANISH CHAIRS

wasted; we listen to blood-curdling tales of the murder, and how the body smelt when it was hidden, and how Sir John, the historian's grandson, confessed to having done the deed—a death-bed confession—when his time for doing more deeds was rapidly passing away. Outside the bedroom door was a secret room behind the panelling. It is now a housemaid's closet, but close the door and lift up boards in the floor carefully, for there is a deep drop, with a Jacob's ladder, down in the thickness of the wall to a depth we cannot fathom. We are told there is a bottom and a passage underground for three miles. It is a gruesome looking hole, enough to make one shudder. Fortunately it cannot speak, or there would be more ghosts to fear when the pale moonlight gleams along these panelled corridors.

There is another secret staircase that has never been opened, a big square of brickwork right up the middle of the house. It might be dangerous to meddle with it, for no one knows what family skeletons may there be hidden and forgotten. One ghost-room is enough, and this one may again be useful; for even a good lord of the castle might have an objectionable mother-in-law, and, if she slept here, the fairies might take her down that long passage to their fairy revels in the park, or in the river that runs beyond the garden.

The state bedroom is a grand example of an Elizabethan state apartment, so crammed with the finest original furniture that we cannot get from it to photograph it. Linen-fold panelling encircles it with Jacobean above, and over that is Spanish leather gilt. Nearly all the best rooms have a deep frieze of this richly ornamented leather, the only fruit that is left of the romantic trip to Spain. There are very curious chairs of various ages, those by the bedside being of black wood, with spiral arms and legs. A

OLD FURNITURE

"bride's chest," dated 1662, and bearing the initials of Katherine Panton. The table is dated 1644, and the bed 1568. It is written Queen Elizabeth and King Charles both slept in this bed; but of course they could not be there together. When she came another bed was prepared for her favourite Robin, with entwined L L and the coronet of an earl, but the panel was upside down and the bed in another room. It was probably only made for show.

The ornamental plaster-work in the passages is very like that at Plas Mawr, and was doubtless worked by the same artist. The chairs shown on page 219 are another lot of Spanish manufacture, and of Spanish leather, 1626 being given as the date of their purchase. Another tradition says, that the oldest parts of Gwydyr House were built by the men who built the first St. Paul's in London; but when every room has a different date to its chimney-breast where the household gods reside, what do a few centuries matter?

THE OLDEST DOOR

Still more fearsome yet fascinating legends tell the spirits of the Wynnes are not yet all at rest.

The next day was Sunday, and we were wicked enough to begin the Sabbath by breaking it—that is, breaking it according to some people's ideas. Our hotel has a famous sign—"The Royal Oak"—painted by David Cox in 1847 instead of an old one and given to the landlady of that day. In 1880 the tenant failed, and £1000 was offered for the sign. Litigation ensued up to the House of Lords, who decided the sign to be part of the freehold. We thought it could be photographed early in the morning before the travellers were stirring, but there was a parson who had gone to early celebration, and another man had an ecclesiastical waistcoat with a big gold cross at his watch-chain, and there were Americans who ended every sentence with "That's so," and the Welsh servants ended theirs with "Yes, yes," and there were murmurs and objections, so we refrained and departed.

We went to church, not to the new fashionable one, but to the old worn-out one, where there is no service, though there is the silent witness of the mounds of mouldering sod beneath the everlasting yews. It was a glorious Sabbath morn, with mists on the encircling hills and the gently prattling river flowing by. I was pleased to find the church door open, and I went inside, never dreaming that I was rousing the ire of X. "What did you go inside for? Did you put anything in the box? It's all superstition—pure superstition, like bigoted church-folk. How much did you put in?" were some of the torrent of his words. I replied by asking what it mattered what I put in. He said it did matter very much, for he should have to put in the same. That seemed very curious superstition to me, and brought up something about a widow's mite, although comparisons are odious and invidious. He

FROM THE OLD CHURCHYARD

THE OLD CHURCHYARD, BETWS-Y-COED

A MUSING ON THE INSURANCE OF TYRES

was determined to start fair, for there was a long day's travel before us, right over the mountains to the western sea, more than a Sabbath day's journey, and it would not be fair for me to try and insure my tyres (this was taking the narrowest view) while the devil could puncture his.

Up one of the most beautiful valleys in Wales—that is, in the world, up the valley of the Lledr, we cycle through hills and woods, by heather and grass, where the mountains come down to the foaming river and the grey rocks shine through the brightest green, where artists paint and artists dwell, we gradually rise to a higher, bleaker land, where the wind blows keener, and we cannot tell whether it is raining or not, for the mists drive down to meet us, blotting out all the landscape and then lifting to give glimpses of miles of mountains.

The lonely ruins of the Castle of Dolwyddelan are on a steep rock by the roadside. The English pronounce this name as if it were Dolly Dillon, with the Welsh it is more like Doll with Ellen. We pass it and turn again, uncertain what to do in the wet. Then we call at a little farm, Bryntirion, where twopence each is charged on weekdays to tourists for the Castle key. We knew the Sunday Closing Act was strict in Wales, but there is something stronger than any Act, and I went to the house to tempt them, while X photographed. A sixpence was soon taken, but the twopence change seemed hopeless, so I offered to take it in milk. The offer pleased the woman greatly, for it relieved her from the difficulty of paying money on the Sabbath. There were a few lean cows peacefully resting in the deserted courtyard of the Castle. I felt inclined to milk one, if it had not been Sunday and they had not looked so poor.

All around were curlews calling—calling, whist-

DOLWYDDELAN CASTLE
The stormy home of the great patriot.

ling, wailing wild and weird music. Shepherds or colliers with dogs were wandering over the hills as if in search of eggs. A belated cuckoo called though it was midsummer day, and wheat-ears flitted from the tussocks of grass. We were cold and wet when I told X there was milk at the farm, but I knew he had had none for years, since one of his crazy doctors had told him milk was very bad for him. We thought of our words at the church in the morning, and if milk was good for me it should be good for him. He gave the woman a shilling and asked for some milk. She brought a pint of it, which he swallowed without a sigh, and said he would do as I had done and take the change in more milk. Then the good woman was like Jael the Kenite, who brought forth butter in a lordly dish, but she also brought plum cake or stodgy dough with currants in it. X tackled the stodge as if he were a police constable, and, when I warned him about it, he promptly gave me the name of another of his doctors, who said currants were the most sustaining food he could have. The dough was enough to choke any doctor, so we buttered it freely and had a good lot of "currant Tommy" for our Sunday dinner, with plenty of milk while we talked to Jael about her tridarn, or three decker oak cupboard, dated 1651, her Welsh dressers with lustre ware, willow pattern old plates, warming pans, copper kettles, chairs, curious hinges, &c.

Let us hope the reader will forgive these petty details of our feasting on plum dough in the heart of wild Wales, on the very spot that should to Welshmen be for ever sacred, where their sleepless patriot, Llewelyn the Great, mightiest of all the Princes of Wales, began his stormy life amid his stormy hills.

Reared here almost in the clouds, exposed to every wind that blows, and free as the mountain air, he must have grown to manhood, strong and healthy. His long

LLEWELYN'S LONELY HOME

red lance and red helm, crested with fierce wolf, towered above men in the day of battle. Warily and well he fought for his country, and, in his day, kept it free. But "the coiling serpent" of the Norman English increased in strength and came again with dragons' teeth among the varying tribes of Wales. What wild excitement Dolwyddelan's Castle saw when Edward's army forced its way in mid-winter over the barren mountains from the vale of Clwyd, up the Elwy River, by Llangerniew to the ramparts of Snowdon, and the grim rocks of Moel Siabod sent on the echoes of the English bugles and the shout of victory into the inviolable sanctuary of the Cymry.

It was in January 1283, there came an exceeding great army—a thousand men from Cheshire, the best archers in the world, before whose yew bows and goose-winged shafts the spearmen of the Welsh were helpless; two thousand more from Salop and the borderland; eight hundred wood-cutters and road-makers, with many Celtic traitors, and fifteen hundred hireling bravos from Gascony and Picardy. Even at this lapse of time there comes a sorrow and a shame that England's King should pay the scum of France to slay his neighbours. He, as a Norman, was more akin to the French and spake their tongue; but we, whose forefathers have lived for centuries by the borderland of Wales, must be kindred with the ancient Britons, whether we like it or not; and, though our speech may be more French than Welsh, we may read in English of "Cambria's curse and Cambria's tears on England's ruthless King."

For miles of desolate moorland road, winding over the mountains towards Blaenau Festiniog, the land of slate, we journeyed steadily on, leaning on our heavily laden bikes as we constantly crept upwards. Then came miles of downhill in a horrible country, where everything was of slate or the colour of slate. We went through straggling streets, apparently full of chapels and ale-houses. The afternoon services in the chapels were in full blast. The doors and windows were open as if they might be blown away with a hearty Hallelujah. X tarried to listen to the singing, while I struggled with directions given in Welsh and English to turn at various public-houses to find our way to Maentwrog. We did

THE COURTYARD OF THE CASTLE

find a quiet inn at Old Festiniog for tea and rest—the Pengwern Arms—by the church and beyond the slaty town. Here X told me how good the singing in the chapels was and what sweet voices some of the Welsh girls had. Unfortunately it had been wasted on me, for my thoughts would go back to the solitude where the curlews vainly wailed around the ruins of Llewelyn's lonely home at Dolwyddelan.

At the door of the inn we were shown our way to

Maentwrog, a narrow lane winding steeply down by the side of the churchyard. We mounted our bikes in a storm of warnings from landlady, bystanders, police, and schoolboys that we could not understand, but we went steadily and carefully on down a steep road that would be very dangerous to those who had machines without brakes. What jubilations there would have been among the elect if misfortunes had slain us. We were travelling on the Sabbath, and were seen to come from a public-house where we had been drinking; but that sweet little cherub that watches over X was taking care of us, and we safely rolled down miles of hills in lovely country until we came to Maentwrog and its little inn, a homely tavern that brought up vivid memories to me.

In the preceding autumn, when X was busy with grouse and guests, I left home one fine morning, took the train to Bala, cycled over the hills to Dolgelly in the inevitable rain of that country, got well wet, and went to bed after "doing" the Torrent walk—six miles in a bath of hot vapour. The next morning was beautiful beyond description. Nothing could be finer than that autumn morning at the estuary of the Mawddach, where the rivers rush between the mountains to the sea. Tranquil in its loveliness it lay at peace, when suddenly there came a bit of life that stirred me. I rested on the bridge, looking up at Cader Idrys, when the roaring of a cow attracted me to its unusual sound. There were evidently family complaints and complications among some black cattle by the river. A big, black bull came to the roadside where two boys were driving a cow towards me. I was afraid the bellowing brute would get on the road, but the road rose to the bridge and the field lowered to the river. As the cow crossed the bridge, the bull swam into the river, without any hesitation. There he swam about below me, who would have given a small fortune for a Kodak. He could not get out at the other side, for there was a steep bank and fence, so he churned and splashed the water into foam as he plunged in again, swimming like a walrus or hippopotamus with the glistening water slipping off his sleek and shiny hide. On a bed of shingle in the stream he bellowed for his lady love, and roared in vexation at his wife, who had been roaring defiance at the stranger. A farmer came along and told me cattle there would often swim the river or even swim across an arm of the sea. The splashings of the bull would fear the "soon," that is the sewin, and the "saumon." My new friend had been in other lands and gazed with me upon the dark amber torrent, where the black bull had his bath, to the brilliant green of the valley winding through the purple hills to the distant blue of the sea. White wings flapped lazily up and down and the whole scene seemed entrancing.

But there came the sound of panting, rapidly increasing into snorts and snaps. Something passed at a terrific rate. A something in leather apparently, but hidden in mud and filth. It had big goggles bent towards the ground, and seemed to notice nothing, but to flee from all things. Its stink was vile. Was this one of the damned? Some lost soul fleeing from the furies through one of the most beautiful scenes that earth could show. Perhaps it was doing penance, trying to shake the remorseful soul out of the afflicted body.

When that "nightmare" had fled away, I went happily on, presently meeting the holiday folk from Barmouth. Here were seven all armed with Kodaks, but if I told them of the black bull further on, they would probably run the other way. Then came walking parties—four young men all stepping together, turning out their toes, very upright and bareheaded. Some yards behind them were three young women, with broadly braided hair and short skirts, also stepping very sedately together. What would happen if the bull came? I remember young ladies who believed that all black cows were bulls and all bulls were mad, but that is long ago. It seems to me the best thing to do at Barmouth is to get beyond it as quickly as possible.

A good road between the mountains and the sea goes northward for Harlech. Along it I had the perfection of travelling for ten miles. The weather was exceptionally brilliant and clear, but little did I reck of what that foretold—the trouble that was to come upon me. At the rounding of the corner, where the waves were dashing far below, there suddenly rose before me the grim towers of Harlech Castle, with miles of sea and hills beyond, the blue peaks of Lleyn rising from the horizon on the left to the great fortress of Snowdon in the midst. Every cottage garden was brilliant with the flowers of the hydrangea, and all around was very beautiful.

I sat in the court of the Castle resting and musing, and thinking of journeying gently on to Festiniog. It became colder and I thought I felt rain, and, on looking over the sea, everything seaward was blotted out with mist. It was time to be going, but the rain descended in a deluge, and never stopped for twenty hours. Several times I sheltered in sheds by the way, but there never was any cessation of the torrent, and I found I was getting wet to the skin, for a cyclist cannot keep dry through hours of wet and wind in hilly roads. The struggle became severe, and I determined to stay the night at the first inn that would have me.

At the little village of Maentwrog I asked at the shop if there was a decent inn, and was told there was one in the street. It was getting dark, and I was thankful. The partial change of clothes always carried on the bike was welcome. I was the only guest for the night, but the taproom filled with villagers, who gave me an arm-chair by the fire; most of them were stonemasons or quarrymen from the slate quarries of Festiniog. They had a great advantage over me, for they talked in Welsh most of the time, putting in bits of English for my edification or to draw me out. The great debate was on that everlasting education question. They spoke uncommonly well of the squire and fairly well of the parson, but were down on their schools. Only one man stuck up half-heartedly for the church. He seemed to be a gamekeeper, and had six glasses of *cwrw* rather quickly. Some tramps in search of work at the slate quarries came in, wet to the skin; they ate dry bread to their ale. There was an old man, his strong son, short but thick set, soon going grey, thoroughly Welsh, and a grandson. I would gladly have stood them something, but ale was the only thing there; we could not talk, and to offer money publicly when not asked might have been to insult them. I had a little bedroom with window open to the street, where all the eaves were dripping and all the spouts were streaming; but in spite of the steady, ceaseless splashing of water resounding around me, I soon was asleep.

The rain was still falling in the morning, and the landlord advised me to go to the Tan-y-bwlch station on the mountain railway about a mile off. Everywhere seemed to be flooded, and from the train there is a wonderful view over the surrounding country. For the first time I saw the Castle of Dolwyddelan, and, although I had booked to Conwy, I alighted at Bettws, for the rain had ceased. At every station were fishermen, anglers wild with excitement, for they said the flood would bring the salmon up the rivers, and there was nought else worth living for.

I cycled on, resting at Trefriw, and had a fairly good journey as far as the very steep hill by Conwy, where the rain came again. Three successive days of drenching made me glad to go home and thankful that X was not with me. We could come again another year if all went well, for I had found castles that were worth the taking.

To return to page 232, where I left off the record of our pilgrimage from Conwy to Harlech. As we passed through Maentwrog I remembered the way by the estuary of the Dwryd, one of the most beautiful roads in this beautiful country. The tide was out, and wild-fowl or sea-birds were clamouring over the yellow sands in the valley, as if inviting us to "come unto these yellow sands." Enormous ferns hung over the road from the banks of the hills on our left. We met four gentlemen riding on good horses. They appeared from their seats to be cavalry officers, and a little behind was one who was evidently a soldier-servant. Perhaps a mile behind came a riderless horse, a splendid black charger he appeared to be, as he galloped past whinneying loudly, and with reins dangerously dangling. Then came a bareheaded man on foot in spurs. "Has he shed you?" I asked, and the reply was, "Yes, dem him."

We arrived safely at Harlech just in time for evening service, but the temptations of the flesh were strong; we must secure beds and supper. It was raining again with a strong wind from the sea, but our Sabbath day's journey of thirty miles over the watershed of North Wales was safely done, and we were tired and thankful. In the twilight we ventured forth across the golf links and the steep and shifty sand-hills to the sea. Old records say the sea once washed the rocks below the castle: in Pennant's time (130 years ago) he described the lowland as a marsh once covered by water. It is traversed now by a railway, and the train crawls along it twice a day for six days in the week. The sand-hills, with their sword-like grass, are the biggest I ever saw ; if it were not for them the sea might some day surprise those idle golfers who foozle and swear in some of the grandest scenery that can be wasted on them.

HARLECH CASTLE

This castled crag of Harddlech has a history worthy of its splendid site. To begin at the beginning, and to be brief. Here sat Bran the King of Britain, on his rocky fortress, gazing seawards as the King of

Ireland sailed up to him with a gorgeous fleet, and palavered with him about his sister, who was noted for her white bosom, though nothing was said about any other peculiarities she might have. A bargain was made, and Branwen, to the joy of every one, sailed to be the Queen of Ireland. But the Irish had always queer ways of doing things, and after a time they were tired of their Queen, and promoted her to be cook. She sent a starling to fly to her brother, and tell him how she was being treated. So he sailed over to rescue her and some one cut his head off, and the head went on talking, although it used to be said that even a woman was quiet when her head was cut off. The head of "Bran the blessed" went to London, where its identity was lost. The starling interests me the most, for when starlings sit near their nest singing their twittering, twattering song, it does sound like a Welsh girl talking.

Edward Longshanks, one of the very few English Kings who was worth his salt, built this Castle of Harlech about 1290, at a cost of £8.167; when Conwy Castle had only cost £7.787; and Conwy is superior to this in every way. The transit, the danger, and the keeping in touch with Harlech would be greater than at Conwy even when the sea came to the rock of Harlech. All that matters nothing now. Are there two castles on this earth comparable to them in majesty and beauty? In ruin as they are, their glory has not departed; it lives in song and history. There is no Ichabod written over their portals, and their beauty mellows with the softening of time.

Glyndwr, the great patriot of Wales, "the damn'd magician" of the English King, "the worthy gentleman, well read, valiant, and bountiful as mines of India" of his son-in-law Mortimer, laid long siege to Harlech, took it, and was beleaguered in it with his family. Mortimer died in it. "Revolted Mortimer," at whose

HARLECH CASTLE

name the "canker'd Bolingbroke" trembled, and Hotspur said—

> "I'll have a starling shall be taught to speak
> Nothing but Mortimer, and give it him."

I wonder whether this starling would be akin to the one noted before. Many starlings might be kept at Harlech with long pedigrees. I did see a boy risking his neck to get a young jackdaw from a nest in the Castle. He said it would sell well when it spoke English—but neither it nor its parents were speaking English when he caught it.

Another name in Harlech's history is Margaret of Anjou, "She-wolf of France," Queen of England, "with tiger's heart wrapt in a woman's hide." Every house for miles around was burnt to cinders, and all the country wasted by the Yorkists. Even here came the great Civil War, and Harlech was long held for the King; but why dwell on this history of bloodshed and strife; all the puppets in the pageant have passed away; the bitter feuds and hates are better forgotten; let nought remain but the Castle; and the song—the battle-song that has outlived its authors and will long outlast even the grim towers of the great Castle—

> "Other nations shall arise
> Heedless of a soldier's name,
> Sounds, not arms, shall win the prize,
> Harmony the path to fame."

The earliest and the finest military march that is known to the world of music or of war is that known as "The March of the Men of Harlech." All memory of its origin is lost. In modern times R. Llwyd wrote that the strains were composed at a siege of the Castle in 1468, when Dafydd, ap Jevan, ap Einion had to surrender to the Earl of Pembroke in the romantic manner related in the guide-books. But those soul-

HARLECH CASTLE

stirring strains do not sound like a surrender and a march out of the Castle.

Pennant does not mention his country's war-song, but he does mention a noted tune, "*Ffarwel Dai Llwyd,*" addressed to the Llwyd of Cwm Bychan, a place near to Harlech, when he marched with his men to the great rising of the Cymry in aid of Henry Tudor, the first King of England who was British by male descent and whose success fulfilled the prophecies of Merlin. The martial music that sends the blood tingling through the veins full of hope and energy was well fitted to inspire and nerve the remnant of the ancient Britons in their march for the invasion of England.

If this great war-song was not created then, it may have been in the fierce struggle against the "ruthless King" who ordered the slaughter of the bards. All records or legends of its creator or its place of birth are lost. Is there in all this "clime of the *forgotten* brave" one bard who can tell the tale in English for those who know that tongue alone?

Here, where

> "The voices of the dead
> Sound like a distant torrent's fall,"

we wonder what the men of Harlech are doing now? Most of them seem to be jerry-builders, though some may be golf caddies. Ugly little houses, like an invading army, are encompassing the Castle roundabout, above, below. Those above may send their sewage down. Those below contribute smoke. There is no beauty in them; the curse of cheapness seems to brood over all. There is constant ringing of the builder's trowel or the joiner's hammer, and the wind shakes the house while we are in bed, though the stately Castle has withstood all the storms of the

Welsh mountains and the gales of the Irish Sea for six hundred years.

> "You have the Pyrrhic dance as yet,
>   Where is the Pyrrhic phalanx gone?
> Of two such lessons why forget
>   The nobler and the manlier one?"

Why forget the art of building? The jerry-builders all around us to-day are mostly Welshmen, and we see few good houses in Wales. The ages of strife in which their forefathers were reared, have probably developed the pugnacity of the Welsh, and caused so many to become footballers, parsons, or lawyers, careless as to their houses or gardens or their ugly chapels.

A Welshman dearly loves to be town-clerk to one of the many councils that recent legislation has created; to use a bit of folk-lore it is then a case of "other men's horses with your own spurs."

> "We will not think of themes like these."

Something in the Castle's air brings back to memory bits of song and verse the mournings and the maledictions of the bards.

> "Weave the warp and weave the woof,
>   The winding-sheet of Edward's race."

But X says he is one of Edward's race, so I had better mind what I say or there will be a winding-sheet wanted for somebody. Edward had a daughter, Joan of Acre, whose husband's grave we saw at Tewkesbury, and they had a daughter who had a daughter, and so on, until in nineteen generations X was produced. All this he has shown me in black and white, and when I remind him that strict genealogists do not count women and fifteen of his descents are through daughters, he triumphantly exclaims, "How can you get on without women?" I will leave that to the genealogists and get on with the pilgrimage.

Going south from Harlech, a few miles of pleasant country by the sea brings us to the lodges and gates of a great estate. The carriage drive is at right angles to the road and goes straight up into the mountains. Its end is lost in the dim distance, and its gradient is as steep as the roof of a house. There is neither shade nor shelter; there are no turns and no beauty. It makes matters worse to say Excelsior, and we can only plod wearily on in silence, musing on the great virtues of patience and perseverance that the copy-books used to say were possessed by so few — is it men or women?

This is the straight and steep uphill drive a mile long to Cors y Gedol—a noted old house grandly placed for those who like to live in solitude on Welsh mutton and gaze over the misty mountains and the stormy sea; but for any one who had to descend to the common world and return home when the day's work was done, the weary way would be a very treadmill. We agreed we would not have the house given to us if we were tied to live in it. A tramway might be constructed with descending loads of stone to haul the master up, but horses would break their knees when going down and break their hearts when going up.

The end of the journey to Cors y Gedol is under an avenue of limes. The name means the marsh in the wood, and some of the walls in the oldest part of the house are ten feet thick with hiding-holes in them. The builders evidently sought a place of safety and went a mile up a mountain, through a marsh, into a wood, to build a castle with hiding-holes.

The passing centuries inevitably brought alterations and additions. Fortunately the later work is dated and fairly good. The gatehouse by Inigo Jones was built in 1630, the porch in 1592, with the arms and initials of Griffith Vaughan, or Gryffydd Vychan, who married Katryn Gryffydd after their parents had for-

THE GATEHOUSE, CORS Y GEDOL

bidden the wedding and told them never to darken their doors again.

The young man wandered about and got drunk until the old man died, and then the young one reformed, got wed, and enlarged the old house in anticipation.

The hall bears the date 1576 in curious old figures above the shield of arms. They may be dimly seen in

THE PORCH

our illustration, but it is nearly impossible to photograph dark oak and whitish stone in a dark room. The motto below the shield is SEQVERE·IVSTITIAM· ET·INVENIAS·VITAM. Perhaps it was in Latin to avoid argument, for at that time if a Welshman were told he would find life if he followed justice, he would be justified in saying that was contrary to his experience.

There is plenty of history to the place, for several of the Vaughans were antiquaries, having little to do

THE HALL, CORS Y GEDOL

in times of peace but study their ancestors. I am rather surprised they owned to an Irishman, but it is written that Llewelyn gave the heiress of Cors y Gedol with all her estates to Osborn the Irishman. They were certainly a lively lot long after that, for I find a nice little tale of what took place at a family gathering. They disputed as to which of them had done the best to get justice or to rid the land of the hated Saxons. "Lo! here is the dagger with which I stabbed the Red Judge on the bench at Denbigh," said Davydd ap Jenkyn ap Davydd ap Y Crach of Nant Conwy. Davydd ap Ieuan, ap Enion said, "Here is the sword with which I slew the Sheriff of Meirionydd at Llandrillo fair." Reinallt ap Gruffydd, ap Bleddyn of the Tower said, "Behold the sword with which I killed the Mayor of Chester when he came to burn my home."

Very desperate deeds were these. What intensely bitter hate from the ranklings of injustice there must have been. What daredevil determination for revenge. To stab the Red Judge on the bench—and escape. Was it the "justice" that was Red?

The Sheriff of Merionethshire that David ap Evan thrust through with his sword in the open street was his own cousin and therefore not English, but the bards made poems to him or his father, and called him a "Saint, a lamb of God," and likened their family to "Angels of God on the waters brink and bulls of battle of the Tribe of Hendwr." Saints and angels and bulls of battle seem a curious mixture nowadays, but we must always allow for poetic license—especially Celtic.

The mutual hatred of the English and the British must have been terrible and devilish, though on the borders they were often kinsmen. To burn the houses built with hard labour, and to ravage and waste the land with the crops was done sadly too often. It seems to me now, in old age, and in cold blood, that if the

TREACHERY

Mayor of Chester or the Lord Mayor of Manchester came to burn my home and ruin me, I would do to him, if I could, as the son of Bleddyn the Wolf of the Tower did to his persecutor in the romantic past.

Here is another bit from the family history of these lively patriots when there was no Englishman anywhere near them. A son of a sister of the tribe was

THE COURTYARD

named Howel Sele, and lived near by. He accidentally met Owen Glyndwr, quarrelled with him, and was killed by him. One version of the tale says that he had quarrelled with Glyndwr before, but the Abbot of Cymmer entertained them in the hope he might reconcile them. They went for a day's sport among the hills, where Howel, aiming at a deer, suddenly turned and shot Glyndwr, who was near to him. Glyndwr's stormy life had taught him to wear mail armour concealed beneath his other clothes, and the links of mail stopped or turned the deadly arrow. Howel was never seen again for forty years, and then it came to pass that one of Glyndwr's men, feeling his end was coming, told of a hollow oak where all that was left of Howel might be found, but whether he had been dropped into the hollow trunk of the tree alive or dead seems to be a mystery still. The ghastly carcase did not hurt the tree, neither did the ghosts that haunted it, for it

CYMMER ABBEY

lingered on four hundred years, shunned and avoided by all, twenty-seven feet in girth when it fell "the spirits' blasted tree."

Very terrible and thorough was the revenge of these ancient Britons. The proudest arms their shield could bear were three heads of the hated English. Saxons they called them, but tourists now are many, and the Royal Cambrian Academy of Art think it more polite or more discreet to use the label "Saracen's head."

The Vaughan of Cors y Gedol, who built the gate-

THE HOUSE OF THE LORD

house, complained of the English Government fining him heavily, though they refused to tell him what it was for. His grandson became Member of Parliament for the county, but the feasting in London was so very different to what he had been used to at home, that he got too fat for the House of Commons, and the big doors had to be specially opened for him. He struggled home to Cors y Gedol with London doctors to take care of him, but they cut out his fat instead of starving him, and so he died at the early age of twenty-nine. If he had never left home he would never have died of fat.

Down the mile-long drive of Cors y Gedol we let the free-wheels of the bikes roll with both brakes on to steady them. Through Barmouth's thronged streets we hurry and turn up the estuary of the Mawddach to the bridge where I had seen the black bull swim the river. Here we leave the road and walk alongside the stream to the farm that is locally known as Vanner, or Y Vanner, but is marked in the maps as Cymmer Abbey. Vanner, I am told, means the house of God, or the holy place; Cymmer is the plural of Cwm, or the junction of two coombs of about equal size. The coombs or valleys are the courses of the rivers Wnion and Maw; and as the scene around them is as beautiful and as fertile as any in this or any other land, those good judges the Cistercians had got some Meredydds and Gryffydds with all theirs aps to grant them a bit of this fair earth that by the sparkling streams they could build for themselves a sanctuary where they might quit the world and worship their God in peace.

Seven hundred years ago Llewelyn confirmed the charter to Esau the abbot, and the monks of Cymmer. Was this Esau a red and hairy man, a cunning hunter, who made savoury meat of venison? for centuries after his day the hills around were noted for their excellent venison. See the house of the Lord to-day. Thorns and thistles grow around it. A big sycamore blocks

THE HOUSE OF THE LORD 253

the door of the church, for the abbey church has literally and actually become a fold for flocks. The bleating of the sheep as their wool is shorn from them is in our

IN THE DOORWAY OF THE CHURCH

ears. The infirm and sickly are locked in the church, and the cade lambs pasture in the sanctuary on the short sweet grass that grows over the graves of those who built it and who rest below it. It may be sad to see the church become a sheepfold, but it might be worse.

All things are slowly reverting to nature, and here there broods a long continued calm decay.

The refectory, where the monks ate, is naturally better preserved than the church where they prayed. On its picturesque steps are lambs chewing their cud with restless lips or querulously bleating—not for their mothers, for they have none, but for the milk they long for. We also would like some milk and we get it in wooden bowls with rims of pewter that would indeed be precious if they were in the curiosity shops or the museums of England.

It seems a shame to take the food of the poor little orphan lambs. It would be better to take their photographs, but there is steady, persistent rain as is usual in this country, and X is careful of his blessed camera. The rain does not trouble me, for I feel like a milk-fed lamb that is full and at rest. Their sweet innocence knows nothing of paschal feasts with bitter herbs or mint sauce. They have heard the milk cans rattle and they baa in chorus till we shut them all up but one, or hold them fast while X takes a hurried snap under the shade of the limes that were planted in the days of the merry King; but not for one-tenth of a second would that one little ewe lamb be still.

Let us leave them while they are happy, for the rain is making the grass to grow upon the mountains, and with more grass will come more milk. There will be plenty for all, and peradventure the salmon are rushing up the river that swirls by the garden wall, and some day the salmon may meet the lamb—but mercy hides the future.

We seek the neighbouring mansion, Hengwrt, that seems to have escaped the pilers up of guide-books, but whose name cannot long escape the man who reads old Cambria's history, for there he will soon read of the Hengwrt MSS. The name means the old court, and the house is built on the site of the abbot's house,

CYMMER ABBEY

and probably many of its stones have been brought from the ruins of the abbey.

The oldest part appears to have been the private chapel of the abbot. It has a beautiful Early English window of three lights, narrow lancets with the highest in the midst, but the place is spoilt by a big meat-safe

A CADE LAMB

that protects the ribs of a cow, or the son of a cow from the blue-bottle flies that buzz around it. Salted swines' flesh in the house of the Lord is rather jarring, but if admirals and archdeacons say it is right we must not rail against dignitaries. The house is to let and the local Mr. and Mrs. Jones show us round. Forgetting he is Celtic, I ask him if there are any hiding-holes, and immediately his eyes glitter with suspicion. It is evident that he takes us for burglars who wish to know

THE STAIRS

where the valuables are kept. He evades all questions, never takes his eyes off us, and watches every movement. Explanations are useless, but we had written leave to photograph.

On the stairs is a massive oaken chair with sockets for poles for carriers. I turned it round to get it in the picture of the staircase if possible. In it the Robert William Vaughan of Hengwrt, who was Member for Merionethshire, was carried about at his elections, for he was another very fat man. The dates on its back are the dates of his elections: they begin with 1792 and end with 1833. It is not stated when he became too fat to walk and the chair was made; let the reader take whichever date he prefers. The child's chair is dated 1669, and the initials may be for George or Gryffydd Nanney.

The Vaughan family have owned the place for centuries. The antiquary died in 1667, and long afterwards some of them always spelt their name Vychan.

The famous Hengwrt manuscripts are taken care of elsewhere, but there are a few antiquities worth noting. One is a spear head that was lately found at a neighbouring farm. In their border warfare the Welsh mainly relied on their spearmen. A large harp may be seen on the left of the fireplace in the hall; it was as mute as if the soul of music had fled. X dare not strike its trembling chords or even touch it, and there was no bard present to fire the patriot's breast, "to melt us to sorrow or madden to crime."

There is a curious heavy cup of bronze inscribed E. R., 1601, that was found built up in a wall, and a bronze pestle is dated 1730, with initials that probably stand for Richard and Mary Vaughan. An oaken cabinet is dated 1639.

When we were there the house was to let furnished, and in all my wanderings I never saw a more pleasant furnished house that was to let. It is an old place in a delightful situation, comfortable and homelike. The

THE HALL, HENGWRT

photograph of the front was taken in heavy rain, though we feared the misty mountains would not show at all.

The rain was so persistent that we went to Dolgelly and took the train to Towyn, securing beds for the night, and then sallied out again to find Llanegryn a lonely little church up in the hills, where tradition says the rood-screen from Cymmer was hidden and preserved.

Anything would be hidden in Llanegryn to-day: how the place was ever found even by wandering Welshmen, when there were no roads or railways, is a mystery. Perhaps they took the screen to pieces, and fastened the rood on to some old goat to see whither he would wander in the wilderness. We wandered in the wilderness and in the wet, pushing our bikes up and down lanes or watercourses, wondering where we were going and what we were doing there. Faith is a fine thing and so is fair weather. What we lacked in one we must have made up for in the other. We found the church and the distant place where they kept the key of the church. The beautiful rood-screen was photographed in the dark by nearly half-an-hour's exposure, X being constantly troubled that I should be shown to be praying in the church, for he said that would spoil the picture, and it would be worse if my ghost was flitting about. The wet was running off me, and, after partly undressing, I had to keep the blood in circulation and pray for something.

The combination of sweating and praying reminds me of my neighbours at the Wesleyan College, Didsbury. Their doctor advised the building of a fives-court where the students might have harmless and healthy exercise and so get into a good sweat; but a stern old Methodist governor said, "If it is good for them to sweat let them pray till they sweat"; he would never tolerate the pastimes of Satan. I was sweating and soaking without the praying, and it seemed little use praying for fine weather in that country. Even my

HENGWRT

friends and neighbours do not get all they ask for in their prayers. When I was churchwarden in 1871 and was consulted by the rector as to whether he should publicly pray for fine weather, I told him the Methodists had done it for several Sundays without the least success. The best way is to take things as they come and be thankful they are no worse.

Our long wet day's work was not done, for we had to wander on and find another old house that was said to be somewhere in the neighbourhood, and somewhere may be anywhere in Wales. X had its name written on a bit of paper, but his writing is more picturesque than legible, and if we made the name out we did not know how to pronounce it, for Welsh is one of the many subjects neglected in our education. The map stuck together with being opened in the wet, and we felt rather sticky all over. The lanes were stony puddles or the beds of waterfalls, and the distance was blotted out with the mist. It was little help to ask the way from geese or sheep, and when we met a wild-looking youth on a shaggy colt, he stared and shouted something like "Dam Saxon," and left us to think about it.

Now that I can write calmly about our travels and try to spell the names of the places correctly—it was Dolaugwyn or "The bright meadows" we sought, and the meadows may be bright if the sun ever shines, for there is plenty of green grass. We had to cross the Dysynni river and go by Bryn Crug up some little Afon, and then by Ynys Y Maengwyn back to Towyn. The reason why we must find this outlandish place or perish in the attempt, was because the maternal ancestor of three generations of men who had served X to the best of their ability, came from there. Her name was Evans, and a Mr. Evans lives in the house to-day, for his big body may be seen blocking up the doorway in the photograph. The house is certainly a curious old house of three hundred years ago, though it looks much

THE ROODLOFT FROM CYMMER, LLANEGRYN

more modern. There are several mantelpieces with most elaborate coats of arms that would doubtless be very interesting to antiquaries. To us they were merely hieroglyphics, though we could read initials and dates. The initials are generally G for Griffith, and N for Nannau. The dates are 1628 and 1656. The stairs are of solid blocks of oak between two walls, with a right angled turn at every few steps, and are therefore a strong tower of defence.

AN OVERMANTEL AT DOLAUGWYN

We were told that Cromwell slept in the house when going or coming from Pembroke, and there is a curious deed of marriage settlement between Lewis Gwynn and Jane Nanney, printed in *Archæologia Cambrensis*, that gives us the date and the builder and his payment in lieu of jointure. It is dated 1620. ". . . to the said Jane for and during her lief in lewe and steed of ioynctuer payable yearly at the newe howse of the said Lewis Gwynn in the parish of Towyn called y Dole Gwyn."

It is an old saying that many Welsh pedigrees go back to Noah and the time of the Flood, and no doubt the Welsh weather often causes many of those who

DOLAUGWYN

endure it to think about Noah and his forty days of rain. They may pray that the Flood does not come in the tourist season, but it is dangerous to rely on the efficacy of their prayers. We had a big hotel to ourselves, and went early to bed and early to rise. It rained all night and deluged in the morning. The year before I had spent three days in the district and been drenched every day. We fled by the morning train through Aberdovey, and along its wide estuary, up the rich vale of Dyfi or Dovey, past the old town and church of Machynlleth, ever rising upwards, leaving the brilliant green grass for the browner moors, and, after slow but steady progress, we descend again down the valley of another Afon, the little Garno, we come to Caersws and Moat Lane, well remembered from the pilgrimages of other years, and we glide for miles down the upper valleys of the Severn, till the name of Montgomery makes X determined to take to his cycle and brave the weather, but he is persuaded to wait until we get to Shrewsbury, and then we do sally forth—tired of the long railroad ride. We did not venture five yards in proud Salop, for the clouds might have been following, watching and emptying themselves upon us. We waited awhile and went home by a later train. The wet followed us home, and it rained for days. I should think it is raining now in the damp but delightful district round Dolgelly.

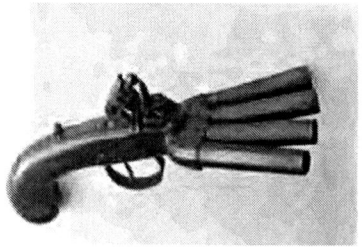

ARUNDEL CASTLE

ONE of the oldest homes in England's long history is the stately Castle of Arundel. It has records for a thousand years, and for nearly all that time we have a continuous list of its lords and valuations of its lands. The Castle itself has grown with the wealth of the nation, but in its round keep there still are remnants of the stonework built in pre-historic times on the steep rock by the river Arun, in Sussex, the land of the South Saxons.

Alfred, the great King, in his will bequeathed Erundellan to his nephew, Athelm. In the time of the Confessor, the Castle of Harundel returned forty shillings for a mill and twenty shillings for pasture; but, when Roger of Montgomery enlarged and strengthened the Saxon's Keep, a borough and seaport were growing round it worth £13 a year. Three hundred years after the Honour, Castle, lordship and borough of Arundel were valued at £600 a year, and in another hundred and thirty years the town and manors alone were estimated at £616 per year. That might be the value of the hotel to-day.

After the Norman Conquest the importance of the place increased, for it lay right in the way of the invaders, and was open to the sea. The Conqueror gave it to his most trusted kinsman, Roger of Montgomery, whose headless effigy we have seen in his abbey church at Shrewsbury, and the picturesque remnants of whose Castle still stand high aloft above the fair] country known as Powysland, "the Paradise of the Cymry."

Roger's son, Hugh, succeeded him, and, like his King, Rufus, who spent an Easter at the Castle, he was shot by an arrow. After him came his brother Belesme, a monster of cruelty, avarice, and lust. He was fitly imprisoned for life, and Arundel was forfeited to the Crown.

As that ends the line of Montgomery, it may be as well to state here that, since the Conquest to the present day, there have been about thirty-eight Earls of Arundel. The historians vary a little, my chief guide being Tierney. If we average the time, there would be about twenty-two years to each Earl on the average. It is not much, but death came suddenly in many ways. The estates do not appear to have been sold at any time, though they were often forfeited or confiscated, and, after many years, restored on payment of fines. Since 1139 or thereabouts, when William de Albini became Earl through his marriage with the widow of the King, they have descended by inheritance, or marriage when the male line failed. After the three Earls of the Montgomery family, came King Henry the First, then five Earls of the de Albinis, fourteen of the Fitzalans, and fourteen of the Howards. They cannot be said to have enjoyed their estates, for if we wade through the melancholy history of our nobles, we must see how little of the noble there was and how much of the primeval savage. Happy would they be who died in battle compared to those whose heads were chopped off in cold blood, or whose years were spent in exile, or in the damp and dreary darkness of a dungeon, where death was welcomed as a deliverance from years of torture.

The history of Arundel Castle is too long for us here. It has had three sieges. The Empress Matilda held it once, and of course it stood a siege in our Civil War, when one hundred officers with a thousand men, two hundred horses, and a great store of arms and

ARUNDEL CASTLE

treasure were surrendered to the army of the Parliament. The garrison were "distrest with thirst, hunger-bitten . . . slid down the walls with ropes. . . . A

THE GATEHOUSE OF ARUNDEL CASTLE

boate made of horse-hides was got out of the castle on to the river . . . but the arch-spie was hanged on the bridge . . . for the royalists in their bloodie crueltie hewed all to peeces one of our wounded souldiers which doubtlesse they would have done to every one of us." A ship from Dunkirk, laden with "brasse ordnance, armes," powder &c., "fell out a fortunate adventure," as she was taken by the Parliamentarians, who thought she was for "the English-Irish that make havocke now in Cheshire." This refers to the massacre of the Puritans in Barthomley Church on the same Christmas eve when the Royalist garrison of Arundel were starving.

Here are the nice old-fashioned names of some of the officers who surrender'd—Shanckes, Reeve, Muckridge, Duellinge, Stitchseame, Cubbe, Hogidott.

For many years after its downfall the Castle was left neglected and forlorn, and would probably have become merely a picturesque ruin, one of the wrecks of time not worth restoring; but its owners had great wealth from land in London, where the streets were paved with gold, and gradually the interest in the old home revived and the Castle grew again, stone by stone and tower by tower, all shapes and styles, incongruous enough; for what is wanted for times of peace is not the same as for times of war, but still the wealth keeps flowing in, and skilled art spends it on Gothic architecture in glistening white stone that every winter's storm and summer's heat will soften into better harmony with the time-worn grey around.

To see and photograph this far-famed Castle we received the kind permission of its noble owner, and duly set forth in a very wet and gloomy morning in July. Half-way to London we found fair weather with the harvesting of hay in full swing. We crossed the great city in a hansom cab, amused at our own contortions, as we constantly expected the horse to tumble down and ourselves to be run over every minute; for the traps and the traffic seemed so different to those of our horsey youth in the long ago. On London's southern side we glided through a calmer country very different in atmosphere of varied kinds from

ARUNDEL

our strenuous north. This seemed brighter, cleaner, chalkyer, hotter, its natives being lazyer, more re-

THE TOWN OF ARUNDEL

spectful, more conventional, with more veneer. At Arundel's little station every one seemed asleep, though they woke up for the moment with the noise of the train; but when that was gone there was the finding and the waking of the coachman to the solitary carriage. He got half-a-crown for driving us two or three hundred yards along the lane through the meadows to the tiny town that nestles under the shelter of the great Castle.

In the course of nature and the fitness of things the best hotel would be the Norfolk Arms, and, though some one had told X of one called the Black Rabbit, he did not desire it. Being safely housed, we strolled round to take a general view of the place before the morrow, with possibly a photograph or two in the bright light of evening. A broad road with avenues of trees and water alongside took us to Swanbourne Lake, encircled with chalk hills, where swans floated on the clear water that reflected mills and haystacks fit for a Duke.

But we were gradually going away from the Castle, so we turned again and presented ourselves at an imposing castellated gatehouse, where we were told that admission to the inner grounds was strictly forbidden, and that was not the principal entrance. The production of an order soon settled that little matter, and when I asked if we could have a guide, a well-groomed man, "all shaven and shorn," of the gentleman's servant class, with a beautiful pipe and a horsey collar, came out quite affably to show the travelling photographers round, apparently thinking he might have his own likeness taken cheaply. As we went on X happened to say something about a letter from the Duke, and the man's hands came out of his pockets, and his pipe went in all smoking hot, his demeanour changed, and, when he had escorted us to the tilting-ground, he formally saluted, saying "Good evening, sir."

The tilting-ground is an elevated, fortified, enclosure, separated from the steep hill of the keep by a narrow, sunken way. It is now a smooth lawn of green

ARUNDEL CASTLE FROM THE RIVER

sward in semicircle surrounded with terrace gardens—an emerald with gems of flowers around, all set in battlements of grey. The rarity and the luxuriance of the vegetation, with its brilliant green, made me forget X and his photography. For the first time I saw the grand-flowered magnolia as a standard tree. The rarely flowering yuccas were in profusion, with enormous spikes of highly scented blooms. Masses of rock-roses with pámpas grass and bamboos were all

THE NORMAN CASTLE

flourishing in the pure air. Elevated and near the sea, yet sheltered by the enclosing walls, it is a charming haven of rest, better for every one than a clashing of knights in tournament.

From the tilting-ground we strolled around the keep and Castle, marking well its bulwarks and telling the towers thereof. We took the inner gatehouse of Norman Roger and the outer one that Richard Fitzalan built just six hundred years ago. Then the few plates we had brought were exhausted, though scores of nature's pictures lay around us. X was so full of the history of the Castle and its keep that had

been bedewed with more tears than any keep in
England, that he waxed eloquent like a parson, and I

THE TILTING-GROUND

naturally went sleepy. Waking up again, I asked
him who his Aunt Eliza was that married the King.
After a little altercation we found that he had been

speaking of Adeliza when I thought he had said Aunt Eliza. Sermons on pedigrees do make me inattentive,

THE NORMAN'S NARROW WAY

but Adeliza is one of his pet ancestresses, a widow of King Henry I. She had no children by Henry, but, after his death, had seven by D'Albini. The King had none by her but lots by other women. That

THE KEEP

is royal license, and he, of course, can do no wrong. One of the King's sons was Robert, Earl of Gloucester, a son of the Nesta who was conveyed with sundry children from Pembroke to Plas Eglwyseg at the World's End in the mountains of Wales. A daughter of the D'Albini's married Roger de Montalt, and brought the breed into Cheshire. X is descended from both of them, but let us be charitable; it is his misfortune, not his fault.

It is said that whoever owns Arundel Castle is Earl of Arundel under a judgment of the King's Council or Act of Parliament of 1433; but another Act, nearly two hundred years later, restricts the dignity to the heirs of the family of Thomas, who was then the Earl. Let us hope that no colossal jobber in dead pigs from Chicago nor dealer in diamonds wrung from the Kaffres will ever have the chance of buying Arundel. Those who own it now have inherited from the Fitzalans, who claim to be descended from the Banquo whose ghost has appeared to most of us, and we may remember Macbeth's horror when the witches showed him the line of Banquo's issue would stretch out unto the crack of doom.

Visions and Romance! Is not enchanted ground with centuries of history the best place for them? As the long setting of the summer sun casts great shadows from the many varied trees across the lawns we sit below a cedar and listen for a sound. The only castle-home that we have seen at all like this is Dunster. Dunster, never bought and sold but once, is more of the mediæval, feudal castle, openly dominating the charming little town and the wild luxuriant country around. Arundel seems more modern than it is, and has to be kept free from the crowds of tourists from London and the southern coasts that swarm around its walls. We felt we were greatly privileged at not only being allowed inside and to photo-

ARUNDEL CASTLE

graph, but being turned loose to go and do as we pleased.

We slowly rambled round the inner park and found

a most beautiful cricket-ground, levelled and sunk like an amphitheatre of greensward encircled by fine trees, with a carriage drive and seats around. Some of the retainers of the Castle were practising at the nets, but we heeded them not, and passing on were surprised to find some recumbent effigies of knights and bishops lying quietly together as in a flower-bed by the path. They were of sculptured stone well wrought in the ages of art, now broken and defaced, with young trees growing among them, pushing them awry or holding them partly erect. Limbs were riven from bodies and mitred heads had fallen down. They seemed to be monuments from ruined abbeys—the images of great men who had taken with them to the grave their honours and renown, and were now forgotten, though their effigies had been rescued from the pillage and laid to rest, with perhaps the bones also, in this secluded park. Some bore shields of arms and some had dresses of the fashion of centuries ago, but there was nothing to say who they were or whence they came, and now the harts tongue fern grows in the stony crevices of the priestly robe, or 'mid the armour of plate and the grey lichens spread on the wan cheek and over the sightless eye.

On the following morning we were at the Castle early, ready and willing to see and photograph some of its many treasures, but to do justice to them would take weeks, and we had merely a few quickly passing hours. There was literally the embarrassment of riches. The most noteworthy works of art in the Castle are the family portraits, but we had not asked to photograph them and therefore refrained. Some are known to the public as the pictures of men whose names and deeds are well known in our history and literature, and as the works of artists whose names and works are perhaps better appreciated than those of the great ones who honoured them with their patronage.

In one room are portraits of Richard III. and the first, second, third, and fourth Dukes of Norfolk. Let us hurriedly learn a little of them. Burke's Peerage begins the lineage of the Howards with Hereward the Saxon and other myths, but Dr. Round says this is a mixture of ignorance and falsehood, and he "rounds" on the imaginations of "Burke." The earliest authen-

THE ENTRANCE TO THE HALL

tic ancestor in the male line appears to be Sir William Howard, who was Chief Justice of the Common Pleas six hundred years since, and whose name had been spelt Haward and le Hayward. From him in male descent, through twenty generations, comes the present Duke, our host. Sir William's grandson, Sir John Howard, was admiral of the fleet in 1335 and became Sheriff of Norfolk. A grandson of this John was also John and Sheriff of several counties. His son, Sir Robert, married the daughter of Thomas Mowbray, Duke of Norfolk (third in descent from Edward I. and his second wife, the daughter of the King of France), and his wife, the co-heir of Richard Fitzalan, fourteenth Earl of Arundel. Here comes in the strain of royalty and the beginning of the family's greatness. The only son was John, who became the first Duke of Norfolk of the Howard family. He was killed at Bosworth with his King and patron, having had notice of the treachery or change of mind of others by a warning fixed to his tent on the eve of the battle.

"Jacke of Norffolke be not to bolde,
For Dykon thy maister is bought and solde."

These lines are older than the lines of Shakspere, who missed a tale he would have liked that is in the chronicles with them. King Richard, suspecting treachery, went eavesdropping on the eve of the battle. He found one of his sentinels asleep, and stabbed him to the heart at once, saying, "I found him sleeping and I left him sleeping."

The second Duke, who was commander-in-chief at Flodden, seems to have died naturally, an ending that was not usual in the family at that time.

The third Duke, whose life-like picture by Holbein as "Marshall and Tresurer off Inglonde" shows him a thoughtful, careful manager and schemer, was a very great man in his day. His first wife was the daughter of Edward IV., and therefore niece to Richard III. and aunt of Henry VIII. His nieces, Anne Boleyn and Catherine Howard, married the King, and had their heads chopped off accordingly. His half-brother, Thomas,

THE GREAT HALL

was imprisoned for life in the Tower, because he wanted to marry the King's niece. His daughter, Mary, was married to one of the King's bastards by special dispensation of the Pope (both Pope and King winking at something when it suited them). His son and heir was beheaded, and he also was to have been beheaded, but accidents will happen, and he was spared to languish many years in prison, for on the eve of the day for execution the bloated King, the Defender of the Faith of the Papacy, the Supreme Head of the Church of England, the Anointed of the Lord, who had long been a festering mass of corruption unable to stand or walk, breathed his last curse and died to the joy of Christendom.

The fourth Duke was grandson to the third, his father having been beheaded, and his turn for the operation came when they accused him of wishing to marry Mary Queen of Scots. His son Philip, Earl of Arundel, thought it better to marry and retire into private life; but the illegitimate Elizabeth never approved of her young courtiers getting married, so he was soon condemned for treason and locked up for life where his wife and children could not see him, and he himself might never know the hour for his execution. As he did not die as soon as expected, some poison was administered in a savoury roast teal that tempted his appetite, and though there is nothing to show the Gracious Queen ordered it, we, who read her letters to the keeper of the Queen of Scots at Chartley, blaming him for not shortening the life of that Queen, know some of her double deceits, and it is recorded that the dying Earl of Arundel asked to see his wife and children for the last time after eleven years of separation, but "Good Queen Bess" said "No, unless he changes his religion." She had him buried cheaply in his father's grave in the Tower, spending ten shillings on a coffin, and the parson who got some black cloth

IN THE DRAWING-ROOM

thanked God for taking "this man out of the world." Now he is styled "The Venerable," and his picture by Zucchero still looks sadly from the walls of Arundel.

It may have been a grand thing to be a Duke in those good old times, but I should prefer the more peaceful present, and feel that it would be better to find something more cheerful to write about.

The finest portrait-picture I ever saw is one by Holbein at Arundel, of "Christine," daughter of the King of Denmark, who was the widowed Duchess of Milan when fourteen years old. When she was seventeen our great King Henry was ready for another wife, and his minister reported that she was very tall and beautiful, "of favour excellent, soft of speech, and very gentle in countenance; weareth mourning apparel." What a charming young widow! and fortunately the bloated brute did not get her, though he sent Holbein to paint her portrait, and doubtless gloated over what is perhaps the finest portrait ever painted; but to the royal offer she replied, "She had but one head; if she had two one should be at his Highness's service." This picture was shown in Manchester in 1897, and, as I have recorded in "Folk-Lore," hard-headed, money-grubbing, suspicious men of business felt at the glass, trying to feel if the woman they saw was or was not warm and living flesh.

The only son of the unfortunate Earl who perished in the Tower, the child he was never allowed to see, naturally shunned politics and religion, devoting his life to the study and collection of treasures in art. His letters about pictures, the prices of them, and the painters of them are worth reading after nearly three hundred years have passed. A Raphael for £130 does not seem extravagant to-day, or a Holbein for 300 guilders. Rubens and Van Dyck were wealthy men, refusing many orders, but they did their best

for the Earl who honoured their profession. There are two portraits by Van Dyck now in Arundel Castle at the end of the dining-room under the Minstrels Gallery (see below). One is of Henry Frederick,

IN THE DINING-ROOM

son of the last Earl; he being the third generation denied the title of Duke of Norfolk, though it was restored to his son. The other picture is of Charles I., and during the five minutes' exposure of the photograph I carefully noted the features of the unfortunate King as shown in a life-like portrait. Handsome,

T

unhappy, shifty, faithless, as if he felt that all were wronging him, though he himself could do no wrong, and that his people merely did their duty in surrendering all for him. His settled melancholy shows his sadness and surprise that subjects should rebel against their King.

The preceding page shows another famous picture, the one by Gwillim Strete of Henry Howard, Earl of Surrey, son of the third Duke. He was a man of learning, fond of arts and arms; a poet who commanded armies and was fond of tournaments. A shield he won at Florence in 1536 is at Arundel now. He had abundant wealth and royal ancestry, perhaps better than the King himself could claim. On his shield he quartered the royal arms, and at once his royal master had him quartered.

How differently we judge offences nowadays. If the ratepayers elect a councillor who goes to a stationer and from a pretty book selects his arms, no one objects, even though he may have taken the royal arms of England, as New York's mayor did for his carriage. Surrey had royal lineage and some right to bear the royal arms: in the truth lay the danger. In few words has Shakspere shown him where he taunts Wolsey with kissing "the brown wench," and the great Cardinal says, "If I blush, it is to see a nobleman want manners." Surrey replies, "I had rather want those than my head." His head was wanted.

Below his picture are two documents in frames. One is a vellum deed bearing his signature; the other is a letter to the Treasurer of the Exchequer from Elizabeth's Privy Council. It is dated the 21st of January 1573, and signed by Cecil, Lord Burleigh; Ed. Charlton, Earl of Lyncoln; Earl of Arundel; Earl of Bedford; Sir Francis Walsingham; Sir F. Knollys; and plain T. Smith—all genuine autographs.

THE LIBRARY

These historic documents speak for themselves, but they are with Sevres and Oriental china that may be priceless, and carved works of art on curious furniture that tantalise us because we cannot learn their history or anything about them. In one of the picturesque recesses of the room is a big leathern trunk studded with brass, and in brass-headed nails are the initials K. R. for Katharine of Aragon, the Queen who mourned she "had ever trod this English earth."

Alongside it, all resting on the floor, were piles of family portraits, and we tried to photograph, but could not get far enough away from them and were against the light.

In another recess we saw with reverent sympathy a picture of the present Duke's mother, with smaller pictures of the dead wife and child. White flowers, apparently renewed each day, encircled them—"the white flower of a blameless life."

From this room opens the library with its carved pillars and roof of mahogany. For nearly forty yards it recedes in the dim light, its many "quaint and curious volumes of forgotten lore" safely ensconced within a network of brass. A lost or forgotten early printed copy of "the first folio" of 1623 was lately found here, bearing the book-plate of Bernard the twelfth Duke. X said it was wasting time and trouble to try to photograph such a dark room; it would take twenty minutes, and if I went about reading the names of the books there would be several ghosts in the picture. But the result is good and neither ghosts nor books appear.

There is a good historical bit of oak-carving fixed to the wall above a nonsuch chest in one corner of the great hall. It came from the board-room of the offices of the Admiralty that stood on the bank of the Thames at Deptford, and bears the arms of Sir Thomas Howard,

A NONSUCH CHEST

Lord High Admiral, who became the third Duke of Norfolk. His brother, Edward, had been made Admiral in 1514, with ten shillings a day for maintenance, diet, wages, and rewards. He sailed at once to meet the French fleet and was killed in a few days after his appointment in a sea-fight at Conquet, Brest. He may have been covered with glory; but had had no time to

THE LORD HIGH ADMIRAL'S ARMS

save money out of his wages and perquisites. The panel at the top on the left has a picture of the famous great ship of that time known as the *Henry Grace de Dieu*. Below the chest is a plain walking-stick with a label tied round saying that with that stick a Duke of Norfolk killed a mad dog that attacked him and his son.

In the appendix to Tierney's history is an inventory of all the furniture in Arundel Castle, apparently taken when the Earl was imprisoned in the Tower by the tyrannical Elizabeth. There are many "hangings of sundry auncient stories," otherwise tapestry. One "peece" is of "the VII. planetts," "three peeces of okes and white horses," "five peeces of the story of King David," &c. &c. "Turkie carpetts . . . great andyrons of yron . . . quishions of crymson wrought velvet . . . bedsteede of wallnut-tree . . . with one counterpoynt of crymson taffeta lined with white fustian . . . cubberds of oke . . . chaiers of oke, blacke lether, and wallnut-tree with marke-tree . . . stooles of waynescotte . . . rugges for blancketts . . . fether-bedds, woole bedds," &c. &c. Some of those "cubberds of oke" may be there now, but the other things are probably dust. Most of the Turkey carpets were sent to London, and Tom Cooper, a servant to the Earl, lost "one covering of imagerye." If valuations of the furniture had been given, "the inventorie indented" would have been still more interesting.

The Court rolls also give some good information as to the government of the town, it being a feudal appendage of the Castle. Brewers are fined for refusing to sell ale at a farthing the gallon, and the innkeepers are fined, and so are the butchers, for making exorbitant profits. If the lord ordered prime cuts and was charged more per pound than poor folk were charged for the shank ends, he could fine the butcher for his exorbitant profits, and the butcher would have to eat humble pie and live by his losses, as folk-lore says he does at the present time.

If any one bought their eggs and butter in the country they were fined for forestalling the market of the lord, and if any one had openly proclaimed themselves to be free-traders, they would probably have been hanged as soon as caught and without trial; but those were the good old times, when the lord even made a profit out of his prisoners and kept them in Arundel Castle in dungeons or cellars which, being modernised

THE STAIRWAY

from the original Norman, make comfortable apartments now for servants, offices, or stores. What a pity it seems to have filled those dungeons with prisoners when good old home-brewed ale was only worth a farthing a gallon.

Prisons and ale remind me that something should be written of the ruins by the river bank, as shown in the picture on the opposite page. They retain their Norman name of Maison Dieu, and were built in 1396 by the Earl for an hospital or almshouse for the relief of the poor and needy, the rules, regulations, and accounts being still in existence. The same Earl also built a college, and appears to have made good use of his money and talents, so they cut his head off soon after the Maison Dieu was finished, and at the great robbery of the charities this almshouse was ruined, although it was built and endowed for the relief of the poor only; and now the poor have to be kept out of the rates instead of from the rents of the lands by which it was endowed. Verily our Pilgrimage to this Old Home has brought before us many wonderful bits of history in the strange fates of the lords and their slaves who built the Castle and dungeons and in them fretted their little lives away.

Painted on panel or canvas may here be seen the likeness of every lord of the Castle for centuries. Only few of these Earls of Arundel died in their home, in their bed, in peace. They died on the scaffold, in exile, in battle, in prison, even in a crusade; in all ways and places, anywhere but on the bed whereon their fathers died. In peace and war they served their Kings and Queens, but those Anointeds of the Lord whose Divine Right could do no wrong, seem seldom to have done right.

How fared the vassals and serfs of Arundel? As late as 1288 the burgesses solemnly declared they

THE RUINS OF THE MAISON DIEU

claimed no liberty but from their lord. That state seems to be slavery. Ages after they had more freedom, but if one bought butter and eggs outside his lordship's lands, he had to pay the fine commanded, on his knees beg mercy, or the Castle's dungeons whence no sighing could be heard were ready; and for those who struggled to be free there was short shrift and a long rope ending with a carcase dangling from the battlements. The poor were more or less provided for down to the time of the absolute robbery of them commonly called the Reformation, when the pauper's badge was first invented for a few. "Say not thou the former days were better than these;" the troubles and perils of all classes to-day are as nought to what they were in "Merrie England in ye oulden time."

Let us, in conclusion, have one grand bird's-eye view of Arundel. I tempted X to try the topmost pinnacle of the tower, from whence he might see the Kingdom and its glory. The job was to get there. Masons were repairing the battlements of the keep, and we climbed up the hill to its walls, trying to find a coign of vantage, and dodging falling stones or mortar that the preservers of the Castle might be showering on us, when suddenly a gentleman appeared asking us by whose authority we were there and what right we had to photograph. I told him our order had been given up at the Castle, but I had a letter from the Duke in my pocket that could be shown when my hands were at liberty, for we had to stick fast to anything on that slippery perch. Again the demeanour changed at once, and willing help was respectfully offered, as a workman was summoned to carry the camera and a foreman to make way for us. We were escorted up ladders and gangways, while the work was stopped as we passed. From the scaffolding on the highest battlement of the keep, that was "bedewed with tears" eight hundred

ARUNDEL

years ago, X took what is probably the best photograph ever taken of Arundel, and we felt that it was something to be treated like modern Dukes, if it was only for a quarter of an hour.

FROM THE BATTLEMENTS OF ARUNDEL

THE HOME OF NOBLE POVERTY
WINCHESTER

FROM the home of the Noble to the home of Noble Poverty. From the home of wealth beyond measure, to the home of the poverty of Job— the journey is short.

"Doth Job fear God for nought?"

We left the lordly little town of Arundel in a motor-car—the first time we had ever ventured our precious selves in the last diabolical invention of our scientific age. We were rolled up and down the little hills of Sussex and Hampshire in pleasant scenery, but as there were no horses to bait, there were no stops to be made and many pleasant bits of country were missed. We did stay awhile at Chichester to photograph the cross, and peep inside the cathedral amidst the customary scaffolding, but our chauffeur was crabby and vexed at the waste of time. He could have gone nearly ten miles in that quarter of an hour.

Along the southern coast the corn was ripening a month before ours: the fields were turning white unto harvest and of a dazzling brightness that ours can never be. Portsmouth came into sight with the low frowning forts that guard our southern shores from foes who might sail up our English channel. Then came Havant, and we turned northwards through a land where the culture of the strawberry seems to be superseding other agriculture. Through Bishop's Waltham there are some very awkward corners, but we had no accidents; we did not even kill a dog or a hen, and had fifty-six miles of a delightful journey on a summer's evening for three guineas.

The ancient and royal city of Winchester seemed to be in a state of great excitement and turmoil about a cricket-match. The hotels were full and overcrowded. The one narrow street of the proud little place was packed with cars, traps, bikes, soldiers, cricketers, clergy, nurses, fishermen, boys and countryfolk of various species. As the city contains a barracks, there are more soldiers than there usually are in an English crowd, more clergy from the cathedral, more tutors and boys from the great school, and more tourists, for there is so much to see; but two carts block the street, and when a traction-engine comes along pedestrians have to flee into shops, and cyclists stand at attention with their bikes on the footpath while the smoking, stinking thing that seems to have strayed from the filth of Birmingham pollutes the select street of the little city.

At the hotel they give us a small book of its history, wherein we find the hostel was originally called the Moon, but it was built anew at the time of the battle of Agincourt, and renamed the George after the war-cry of that famous victory. In 1417 the rent was £7, 10s. per annum, but the Wars of the Roses made bad times and the city became the owner, and the rent went gradually down to £3, 6s. 8d. The author carefully abstains from saying the present value of the place, or my former remarks on the value of land doubling with every generation might have been corroborated again, notwithstanding there being many generations in four hundred years.

As X has had several sons at the College, he is quite at home at Winchester, and regales me with tales of his ancestors who were the Kings of early England a thousand years ago, and whose bones, or some others like them, are stored in chests in the cathedral and

THE CROSS, CHICHESTER

put on high screens to keep them out of the damp, for they might spoil if they were in the ground. Some one shook hands with Cnut not long ago, and condoled with him on the obstinacy of the tide and

THE WEST GATE, WINCHESTER

the waves that would not be still. I shook hands with Tom Sayers in my young days, but those fighting men are not so interesting now. However, we determine to go to the cathedral on the morrow, if only for a few minutes, to pray that the sins of the ancestors of X may never be visited upon him or upon his children. "A furore Normanorum Domine libera nos."

THE COLLEGE

The following morning was dull, damp, drizzly, and dark. The east end of the cathedral was like a builder's yard, and, to add to the gloom, X told me the round table of King Arthur was in the Assize Courts. If it be the famous round table, or even a young one off it, how much more at home it would be in the peace of Glastonbury than perishing with

THE COLLEGE, CHAMBER COURT

the jargon of a court of law. We did not waste time on it, but went to the College and photographed the cloisters where they bury the good boys who die at school.

The chief goal of our pilgrimage was not the ancient and once royal little city of Winchester, with all its teeming history, but the Hospital of the Holy Cross, alias the Almshouse, or Home of Noble Poverty. There they give the weary wayfarer bread and ale "free, gratis, for nothing." Much people would walk many miles for that, and although we had driven to the

Hospital and were not very footsore, I asked for my dole and got it, much to the disgust of X, who was shocked at my drinking from a horn-cup that other sturdy beggars had used—"supping swipes" that were certain to make me ill on the way home. But it takes a deal of talking to stop a man from drinking, and I reverently ate my dole of bread and drank the cup of barley-wine in remembrance of the Home and its Founder.

Then we went to church, which was obviously the next thing to do, and just round the corner there stood a constable. Then I felt puzzled and rather guilty. What connection could there be between the church and the ale and the police? It was not a public-house, but there was ale, and it was good. A tired traveller might try for more than his fair share, and the constable might be ready to pounce; or he might be thirsty himself, and solemnly swear that he was a weary way-wanderer. I had about half of a half-pint of good ale in a little horn. The old statutes say that three bushels of malt should be brewed to the hogshead, and that should brew good liquor. I quite agree with restricting the quantity of it, but the quality should be the very best—pure malt and hops—ale that can be brewed, so that every one who tastes it may take it for his standard, and tell his brewer or publican he wants ale like that which is given in charity at the Hospital of the Holy Cross.

To go back to the church. The church is not large, but it is lofty and a splendid specimen of round-arched stonework, now painted over with zigzag bands of colour that give a strange effect. It is very striking, pleasing to some, horrid to others. To me the architecture is majestic, and the whole building pleasing and impressive in its transition from pure round-arched Norman in the east end, to the beautiful Early English of the west end.

THE COLLEGE CLOISTERS

One of the brotherhood of Noble Poverty, clad in a long garb of rusty purple—a survival of the Middle Ages—in the accents of a gentleman, volunteered to show us the treasures of the hall and its surrounding homes. To our hurrying mode of life he seemed too slow and too deliberate, for it may be time hung heavy on his hands, and any attempt to quicken him was like pricking a worm to make it crawl faster, he would impatiently speak of patience, and hesitatingly begin again at the beginning of his tale. It seemed to give him special pleasure to translate and explain the varied letterings of "Dilexi sapientiam," the pious maxim of a pious master, Robert Sherborne, who, four hundred years ago, loved wisdom, or thought he loved it, and unnecessarily proclaimed it in a foreign tongue.

When we came to the hall I saw it was worthy to be photographed, and would require five minutes for exposure in addition to the fixing of the camera, and therefore we had better get to work at once and hear the tale while we were waiting. We thought of saving time, but our guide, philosopher, and brother would be no party to the miserable wickedness of saving time; his self-respect was ruffled, and he rejected with scorn a half-crown that X offered to him, told him to put it in the alms-box at the church, for he, in his Noble Poverty, could not accept gifts from any one. We thought he was rather a peppery pauper, one who had seen better days, had had losses, and remembered some Latin, therefore a good sample of genteel poverty.

It was well we had hurried with the picture of the hall, for before we had finished, modern waiters came with modern things for a modern meal in the old refectory. There are extraordinarily rough, primitive chairs on the dais with black-jacks, candlesticks, and salt-cellars of the time of the Cardinal. On the newel post of the stairs is a pelican vulning its breast,

A CORNER IN THE CITY

but, unfortunately, these things are too small in our photograph and we had only two unexposed plates with us. The original fireplace in the centre of the floor should be noted, for very few indeed are the central fireplaces that have escaped the destroyer. For lack of a guide and time we never saw the interior of any almshouse, but their picturesque chimneys are seen on the left of our photograph, the hall being in the middle and the grand gatehouse of the Cardinal to the right. On this tower are said to be the sculptured heads of the Cardinal, his father John of Gaunt, his mother Catherine Swynford, and the King. He gave his mother all the honour he could, though the uncommon good might scoff, and it seems to me probable this saved the charity in the great day of robbery, for even Henry VIII. might have more respect for these his own ancestors than he had for his wives and their relations or for the charities of others. It showed one of the family had once given something.

The Hospital of the Holy Cross has a strange, eventful history, a history that is more than usually difficult to read aright, for historians are loath to write the truth of dignitaries who might ban their books and get them into trouble, and this charity has been so often robbed by the priests who should have preserved it, that the truth is glossed over, and the plunder left with them, while the poor have been sent empty away.

By chance it happened a few years ago that the Charity Commissioners sought information about a plot of land at Didsbury, called the Poors'-field. There were three acres vested in the rector and churchwardens, and they not liking to be troubled with worldly things sold the field for £120. I objected to the sale, and the charity was preserved under other trustees. The plot is now divided into allotment gardens, brings a gross rental of about £18, and the tillers of the ground derive quite as much benefit as the receivers of the

THE HOME OF NOBLE POVERTY

charity. Then I was asked to be on the Board of Mayes's Charity in Manchester, where the value of the estate is increasing tenfold. With this knowledge I thought the best history of this Home of Noble Poverty might be found in the dry reports of the Charity Commissioners, and, studying them, I was soon immersed in shoals of details.

St. or Holy Cross Hospital was founded anew by Bishop Henry de Blois, a grandson of the Conqueror, and a legate of the Pope. There are no records of the earlier house, but wealth wrung from the conquered English re-endowed this hospital for the poor of Christ; that thirteen poor and impotent men reduced in strength, should there remain with necessary clothing, suitable beds, wheaten bread, &c., and a hundred other poor men of good conduct have what is left. "If any person . . . diminish the said rents or disturb the customs . . . let him incur the anger of Almighty God and the Bishop of Winchester and of all good men . . . to you benefactors of the poor . . . may there be peace and mercy from the Lord Jesus Christ."

For three hundred years, with varying fortunes, this Charity struggled with the spoilers, litigation, and appeals to Rome; then came the great Cardinal Beaufort, who added the almshouse of Noble Poverty for poor gentlemen, and endowed it with enormous wealth. Some of this wealth was lost in the Wars of the Roses, but the greater part is saved and grows in value day by day. There are thousands who never heard of it, though they have read and been fascinated by that vivid scene in Shakspere of the Cardinal's death. Of course, we are told this death-bed tale isn't true, that Shakspere did not write it, and nothing is true. The enmity between the Duke of Gloucester and the Cardinal was well known. The Duke had called him a bastard of his grandfather, and was soon after found dead in his bed, believed to have been strangled by the emissaries of the powerful and wealthy Cardinal. Then to the Cardinal in delirium on his death-bed enter the King and earls—

> "*King Henry VI.* How fares my Lord? speak, Beaufort, to thy sovereign.
> *Cardinal Beaufort.* If thou be'st death, I'll give thee England's treasure.
> Enough to purchase such another island,
> So thou wilt let me live and feel no pain.
> .   .   .   .   .   .
> Bring me unto my trial when you will.
> Died he not in his bed? Where should he die?
> Can I make men live, whe'r they will or no?—
> Oh! torture me no more; I will confess.—
> Alive again? Then shew me where he is;
> I'll give a thousand pound to look upon him.
> He hath no eyes, the dust hath blinded them.
> Comb down his hair! Look! Look! It stands upright,
> Like lime-twigs set to catch my winged soul!—
> Give me some drink!—
> .   .   .   .   .   .
> *Warwick.* See, how the pangs of death do make him grin.
> *King Henry.* Peace to his soul, if God's good pleasure be.
> Lord cardinal, if thou think'st on heaven's bliss,
> Hold up thy hand, make signal of thy hope.—
> He dies, and makes no sign. Oh God, forgive him.
> Forbear to judge, for we are sinners all."

Forbear to judge. At times we have to judge, but we can try to do it fairly. Which did the greater good—the delirious dying man, or those who watched him die? The King tried to be a Christian, and found it impossible to be both King and Christian, so they murdered him also. The earls loved fighting and enjoyed the lives of bulls and cocks. After five hundred years these crumbs from the Cardinal's Charity are doing good. There is no need to pry into his life or the means whereby he got his enormous wealth. I should have liked to photograph his effigy with its hooked nose and gorgeous scarlet robe, but the great cathedral was in danger of tumbling on him, and we could do nothing, for even his tomb was half hidden with scaffolding.

If we turn again to the dry reports of the Charity Commissioners, we find that at the end of the seventeenth century a "Consuetudinarium" or report on the customs relating to the disposal of the funds of the Charity was drawn up, wherein it was stated that the master should receive all surplus rents and profits to himself after paying a steward and a chaplain and keeping thirteen poor brethren; also finding food for forty (not a hundred) in the Hundred Hall. This seems to be an impudent assumption by the master of any increase in the rents or profits from a decrease in the number of paupers.

Each brother's allowance was to be a pint of ale and a piece of bread at eight for breakfast, a quart of ale and a piece of bread at dinner, a pint of ale and a piece of bread at three, and a quart of ale and a piece of bread for supper. That seems rather monotonous, especially if anything went sour, but there were forty-six and a half pounds of beef and the same of mutton every week, which would give one pound a day to each brother, including fat and bone. Milk pottage at times. On Gaudy-days—or festivals they had extraordinary commons with a charcoal fire in the centre of the hall, round which they sat with extra quarts of ale and mince pies made from legs of mutton, currants and raisins, nutmegs and ginger, cinnamon and spice, and all that is nice. Also plum broth, a mysterious decoction for which no specification is given. On Shrove Tuesdays they had pancakes, of course, and roasted hens with extra drink. Pies with twenty-four herrings baked in them for Lent. Honey-sop on Good Friday; this being three pounds of honey boiled with bread in their pot of ale; but if this means that each poor brother had three pounds of honey boiled in his ale, it is evident his digestion had not been weakened by tobacco.

The Hundred Hall poor were fed on sheep's hinges, gurdions, boiled peas, bread and ale; milk pottage on Fridays. A barber was paid three shillings and fourpence per quarter for tittivating the lot, shearing and shaving by contract. Every brother at every Christmas could have a new gown made of black cloth rash at five shillings a yard, but he must go to prayers twice every day in the church; and, lastly, I note the ominous warning that if a brother misbehaved the steward would sconce his commons.

To turn to the more prosaic details of finance. The income of the Charity at the time of the Cardinal's death is given as £458, 13s. 4d.: a rough guess at the wages of a labourer at that time would be a penny a day—that is, if he got any wages. In 1835 the revenue was returned at £1088, 2s. 9d., from which there were many deductions, and the startling statement was soon made that the estates were worth £10,000 a year. Where was the money going? Times were bad; "the hungry forties" came when famine stalked through the land. Returns were made to the House

THE CROSS, WINCHESTER

of Commons, litigation began, and it was proved that for many years the masters had let the properties of the Charity on long leases at considerably less than they were worth, upon payment of a sum of ready money called a fine, which fine they pocketed for their own use instead of spending it for the benefit of the poor.

The Earl of Guilford was the master when affairs came to a crisis, and he appears to have pleaded in the Law Courts that the Charity was an ecclesiastical benefice and therefore beyond their jurisdiction, and to have reversed his plea when before the Ecclesiastical Courts. The Master of the Rolls, in giving judgment, said: "The shameless perversion of one of our noblest charities has been done under a system which not even the most unscrupulous cupidity could have carried out until hardened into a contempt for common decency."

The noble Earl's plunder is variously estimated at sums up to £90,000. Very little was disgorged, and the costs probably came out of the estate, though there is an entry of the defendant paying £1, 12s. 4d. Who was the noble Earl and what was his pedigree? Judges of live stock and of men inquire about pedigrees.

In the sugared and buttered pages of the peerage, one may read of the enormous and overflowing virtues of the Norths. They were mostly lawyers and parsons, who fattened long ago upon the charities and the religious institutions, and stuck to them as if they had been bred for the job. The first Lord North was a lawyer, who became Treasurer of the Court of Augmentations, a new office dealing with the spoils of the religious houses. He received large grants of land from Henry the Eighth, and kept in favour with Edward the Sixth and Queen Mary, therefore his religion must have accommodated itself to that of his sovereigns. The eighth Lord North, second Earl of

Guilford, was the Prime Minister who mainly caused us to alienate and lose the United States of America. He had made his brother a bishop when only thirty

THE FOUNDER'S CHANTRY, WINCHESTER CATHEDRAL

years old, and Francis, the son of that bishop, was made rector of the rich livings of Alresford with house, glebe, and fees, from which he is said to have drawn over £80,000; of St. Mary's Southampton, ditto £120,000; Master of St. Cross Hospital, and Prebendary of

Winchester. The receipts of this pluralist rector were reckoned to be over £300,000. His father's rewards as bishop of the rich see of Winchester for forty years were said to be even more, yet the family motto says, "La vertu est la seule noblesse." Family mottoes are sometimes shockingly sarcastic.

The pluralist rector became the Earl of Guilford, a Peer of the realm, Right Honourable, Most Noble, and a Reverend Priest of the Church, also Master of Arts, but he artfully and, to use the words of his Judge, shamelessly perverted this noble charity for forty years. Will some future poet write of him as Shakspere wrote of the man who founded the Home of Noble Poverty? We may well wonder if these priests "feared God for nought," or was it their poor who got the nought?

In the beginning of this the twentieth century there began a new scheme for the management of the Hospital of Holy Cross, under the approval and direction of the Charity Commissioners. It begins with a very great wrong, otherwise it seems to be well and carefully planned. The first clause recites that every trustee shall be a member of the Church of England, including even the representatives of the Winchester City Council, and they shall sign a memorandum to that effect. The Right Honourable G. Shaw Lefevre (now Lord Eversley) strongly complained of the secrecy and haste with which the new scheme, wholly alien to the principles of modern legislation, had been adopted; but others wrote letters saying that Churchmen's gifts belong to Churchmen, not to those who pick their pockets, and the founders of the charity would have called themselves Priests "Ecclesiæ Anglicanæ." Our retrogressive Government of 1900 appear to have taken this view and published it. Let us look carefully into it. Bishop Blois was a Norman, a grandson of the Conqueror, who would look upon England as a conquered province, and know nothing of the English language or the Church of England. He was also a Legate of the Pope. Cardinal Beaufort was also born in Normandy, and a Cardinal of the Roman Catholic Church. They left the charity free to all. I cannot find any restrictions as to faith, race, or language. If there had been any, they would doubtless have favoured their own. Roman Catholics founded and endowed the Charity, and priests of the Church of England, with "contempt for common decency, shamelessly perverted it," to use the measured language of the Judge. The rich "perverted" from the poor and showed by example and by preaching how the wicked "doth ravish the poor when he getteth him into his net." If in those days the poor had "perverted" from the rich, they would have been hanged without much waste of time.

The impartial records of the Charity Commissioners are my chief authority, and I have always been, or tried to be, a member of the Church of England, though it suffers in this parish of Didsbury the "cure of souls" to be publicly advertised for sale by a speculative draper, and the right of saying who is to be our "Successor of the Apostles" to be bought and sold at a draper's shop, where, at stated intervals, they make "Alarming Sacrifices" and sell flannel petticoats, shirts, stockings, stays, and baby-linen cheap.

The priest who profits by this traffic in the rents and the offerings in the house of God can hold them even against his patron's request to resign. "Intoxicated with the exuberance of his own verbosity," he soon deems himself infallible, and the shorn flock must suffer or seek elsewhere another fold.

Let us turn again to the new scheme for the management of this Charity, hoping and trusting that in the future it may be free from the filtering fingers through which it has hitherto been drained.

The brethren are divided into two classes. The brethren of the Hospital of St. Cross shall not be less in number than thirteen; they shall be poor men who are sixty-five years of age at the least, not in receipt of parochial relief, and so reduced in strength as not to be able to work. The brethren of the Almshouse of Noble Poverty shall be poor men who are sixty years of age at the least, not in receipt of parochial relief, and who have been reduced by misfortune from independence to poverty. The definition or qualification seems to be fair and right. I tried to find any remarks about the daily dole, but it appears to have been purposely omitted as it is "a ticklish thing to tackle."

In a few more years the income of this Charity must be greatly increased, as the leases run their course. It may be multiplied manyfold as the years roll on, and other homes should be built in the place of those that have been destroyed through the carelessness and the greed of the masters, whose duty it was to preserve them. The quad may rise again with cloistered walk for the tottering feet of the poor old men who here are privileged to end their days in plenty. In "the studious cloysters pale" are shade and shelter in all weathers; the green fields lie around, the clear waters of the river are gently gliding by, and distant hills encompass all the tranquil scene.

The good things here offered are offered to the wide world. There are no restrictions as to country, colour, or creed. Wherever there are poverty-stricken gentlefolk with their dim eyes and quiet mien, here is a Home for their Noble Poverty, a garb of faded purple with a silver cross upon their breast. Other Homes there are with sabler cloak, for those whose only glory lay in their strength, and whose fortune came more from

HOME

their muscles than from their brains. Now their strength is hunger-bitten and their force has failed, they may here find rest and peace, if only for a little while. "The brethren of the poor hate him," but "the poor shall not always be forgotten." To all here, but especially to those who have known the sorrow's crown of sorrow, the remembering happier things, we say Farewell.

A COTTAGE HOME

STONYHURST

STONYHURST HALL, the old home of the Shireburns or Sherburnes, has been built or rebuilt and enlarged so often, has known the extremes of wealth and poverty, and is itself known to the uttermost ends of the earth, that one hesitates as to where to begin, or where to plunge into its varied history.

For the last century it has been used by the priests of the Society of Jesus as a college for the education of the sons of gentlemen, and from its "Centenary Record," a book written by Father John Gerard, S.J., I have derived a great part of this account. Father I. Pinnington, S.J., escorted us about the place, and troubled himself with us on the day we prowled around.

Stonyhurst is in the north-east of Lancashire, on the border of Yorkshire, in a grand situation dominating the country round for miles. In many features it reminds one of its neighbour, Houghton Tower, an older, fortified, baronial hall, that is pictured in our previous book. Here we are four hundred feet above the sea, and in its brief summer the scenery is beautiful and the verdure luxuriant, for round about are rivers and hills, and the natives say—

> "The Hodder, the Calder, the Ribble, the rain—
> All meet together in Mitton domain."

Stonyhurst is still in the parish of Mitton, though the greater part of the parish is in Yorkshire. The first mention of the name is in an undated deed

IN MITTON CHURCH

(probably *c.* 1200) wherein Hugh de Midtun conveys all the lands of Stanihurst.

In 1372 a licence was obtained for an oratory in the house, and shortly after the owner's name was Richard Shirburn. In the fourth generation from him came Hugh Sherburn, whose name is on the Minstrels Gallery (page 343) with the date 1523. His grandson, Richard, who owned the estates for more than fifty years, began to build the front and the court that are still the main features of the house. That was in 1592. As in the oft-told tale of folk-lore, he died long before the place was finished, but not before he had built a "new quere" or chapel to Mitton Church as a place of burial for the family. The effigies of himself and his wife, as there they lie in state, we here record. The inscription says: "Here lieth the bodies of Sr Ric'rd Sherburne Knight Mast^r forster of ye forest of Bowland Steward of ye Master of Sladeburne Lieutenante of ye Ile of Man ... 1594."

The figures on the side of the tomb shown on the opposite page, are three daughters displaying the impaled shields that commemorate them and their partners in arms.

This Sir Richard was an important man, who did great things that were contradictorily reported by his historians. Some say he was a Catholic; others say he was a Protestant and suppressed "Wakes, bull-baitings, minstrels, and other disorderly customs." Nowadays the wakes is the great holiday of the year in Lancashire, for all work ceases for a week, and the people migrate to the seaside, where minstrels are not considered to be disorderly customs. Sir Richard's chief work is the entrance or gatehouse with its four courses of classical columns, one above the other, each course being of a different order. The steps into the quad or court are probably modern.

Another Richard succeeded to the family estates

THE SHIREBURN CHAPEL, MITTON

and yet another. Each one plodded at the building of the great mansion until there came rumours of wars and war itself, when all building ceased throughout the land, for who would labour to erect a house that any day might be a centre and a target for civil strife.

Stonyhurst had its great day of anxiety, though no harm happened to it; indeed it gained historically, and its hall table, having been used as a bedstead by Oliver Cromwell, becomes famous evermore, and henceforth its heavy oak is worth its weight in money. This table is shown on page 343 below the Minstrels Gallery. There is no improbability in Oliver sleeping on the table. He was better on a dry table than in a damp bed. I have more than once known guests in an hotel sleep on the billiard tables when there has been a rush of visitors.

Tradition says the table smells of him still. Boys who are in disgrace have their meals by themselves at Oliver's table and they say it stinks; but their appetite is not spoiled. The aroma is not exactly like that of onions or of bitter herbs, but more of the rose-leaves of the poet's vase—

> "You may break, you may shatter the vase if you will,
> But the scent of the roses will hang round it still."

And the scent of Oliver, like the scent of the roses, lingers there still—a sweet-smelling savour for ever.

In the summer of 1648 Cromwell hurried from the siege of Pembroke Castle towards Scotland, with enemies in all directions. What a journey he must have had over those Welsh hills without railways, roads, or even bikes. He got into the north of Yorkshire before he heard that the Duke of Hamilton with more than twenty thousand Scots was pouring down Lancashire to the help of the faithless King. Leaving his cannon and hurrying "very sore every

THE GATEHOUSE, STONYHURST

day" over the hills he bivouacked at Otley, Skipton, Gisburn, Stonyhurst Hall. The distance marched on each day seems small, but the roads were steep and the baggage heavy. At Stonyhurst, on the 17th of August, the whole army of 8600 men was quartered in the field by the hall. The enemy were known to be three times their strength, but Cromwell's advice and orders were like Nelson's long after him: "To engage the enemy to fight was our business." The army had not rested, but early in the morning, the stern old soldier gave the order—"March"! "Our rest we expect elsewhere."

Wherever this great bugbear of the Royalists went, tales were invented about him, and at Stonyhurst he is said to have aimed a cannon shot himself at the cupolas on the towers but missed. Unfortunately he had no cannon and the cupolas had not been built.

Very little is known of the Richard Sherburne of Stanihurst, Esquire, of the Civil War time. Another Richard and another came and went. A grandson, Sir Nicholas, became a great man and the last of his race, for he began to build and make the family mansion grander than ever it was before, and though he did not die before it was finished, his only son died, and the delight of the eyes perished.

The death of this boy is often said to have been caused by eating the berries of yew. Many children eat yew berries, or the pulp off them, without any ill effects, and the death of this boy was in June, when there would not be any berries. The sexton of the church told us the plant sculptured on the tomb is believed to be the mezereum, whose fragrant flowers are common with us early in the year. For his epitaph his father erased Sherburn and wrote Shireburn.

Sir Nicholas laid out elaborate gardens with summer-houses, labyrinth, fountains, shady walks, and many

THE REFECTORY

statues. He bought a thousand yews for £16, 13s. 0d., and paid £2, 7s. 0d. to gild the eagles that look so picturesque above the garden-houses. Grecian gods and goddesses were made of lead, and back to pigs of lead they went again when money became scarce. The contract for the building of the cupolas with the finishing of the battlements and the building of a wall, including all the getting and dressing of the stone, only came to £50. A good architect might charge that nowadays for looking at the job. The leaden downspouts in the courtyard are stamped with the armorial bearings of the family alliances of the Shireburns, and a big new shield for the front door with the family motto cost £30.

Sir Nicholas sent his only daughter to St. Germains "to be tutched for ye King's Evill" by the abdicated James II. His touch was supposed to cure her of the evil, not to give it her. The charges from Stanyhirst, including the King's "phisitian" were £368, 13s. 0d., an enormous amount at that time.

In the Jacobite rising of 1715, the Shireburns were on the side of the white cockade, and the doors of Stonyhurst were shut in the face of the officers of Hanoverian George. Many years afterwards, when some of the older buildings were being demolished, sundry secret and forgotten closets came to light. One of them contained ninety guineas of the reign of James II., a bed, and a bottle of rum. In another were thirty guineas of the same reign. A third had hidden seven horse pistols, the butts loaded with lead, some ornamented with silver, and some thought to be stained with blood. There were other hiding holes about this big house, for they were very useful in the good old times. There the Jacobites met about the time of Preston fight, sat up all night making leaden bullets, and drinking the health of the King—

"God bless the King, I mean the Faith's Defender,
And God bless—no harm in blessing—the Pretender,
But which Pretender is and which is King,
God bless us all—that's quite another thing."

Sir Nicholas, the last of his race, was a Grand Seigneur, who lived in great style, though he kept

A GARDEN-HOUSE

accounts most carefully. When he bought land "dearer than two Eges a penny . . . Deo Gracias," he was thankful for the good investment though he could not foresee that land would be constantly rising in value while eggs could be imported from anywhere. He spent £350 on part of his daughter's "Weding Cloathes" when she became Duchess of Norfolk, and £12, 10s. 0d. for "Sinior Nicolini" to sing.

From the extraordinary epitaph on Sir Nicholas, we may learn that "he did a vast deal of good" in setting his neighbourhood a spinning and combing of wool, and giving them wool and wheels to set up for themselves. His lady kept an apothecary's shop in the house—but that was a dangerous blessing. He was buried at Mitton in 1717, and the estates, after his daughter's death, went to the Welds, the offspring of his sister.

A Sir Humphrey Weld, Knight, was Lord Mayor of London in 1608. He had married a Protestant heiress, who wished to be buried "six feet deeper than her Popish relatives." (Why?) Their great grandson married Elizabeth Shireburn, and they had a great-grandson named Thomas Weld, who owned Stonyhurst in 1794.

Let us now hark back to a more troublous time, two hundred years earlier, when Elizabeth was Queen of England and at war with the Catholics, for they said she was illegitimate and had no right to reign; her reply to them being banishment, fines, torture, or death. About 1592 the English College of St. Omers was founded for the education of the sons of English Catholics. Although it was made high treason for parents to send their children there, and the boys themselves were liable to arrest and imprisonment, the school grew and prospered.

In 1762 the Society of Jesus, who had governed the College, were suddenly expelled from France, and the masters with the boys fled to Bruges in the Netherlands. They appear to have got "out of the frying pan into the fire," for, after eleven uncomfortable years at Bruges, they had to flit again. The Faithful were now quarrelling among themselves The Pope suppressed the Order of Jesuits, sequestrated their property, and authorised the States to seize it. The Government attempted to carry on the College

STONYHURST

for their own benefit, by placing Dominicans instead of Jesuits as tutors for the boys. But the boys re-

IN THE COURTYARD

belled. They wriggled like eels that object to be skinned, and the soldiers were sent for to make them be quiet. From the soldiers the boys would be likely to learn lessons in naughtiness instead of the politeness tempered with Latin that they learnt from the priests. Their parents came for them, and again the school dwindled until a remnant found a haven at Liège, where a Prince Bishop could give some protection, and the College struggled on for another score of years.

Then came the deluge of the French Revolution and again the priests had to flee, for Church and State do not agree in or near to France. The notice to quit was urgent. Brotherhood or Death. Where is the brotherhood to go? From England, "land of liberty," they had fled for two hundred years, but they were English still—

> "Breathes there the man with soul so dead,
> Who never to himself hath said,
> This is my own, my native land!
> Whose heart hath ne'er within him burn'd,
> As home his footsteps he hath turn'd,
> From wandering on a foreign strand!"

Masters and scholars, priests and pupils packed up their little luggage in a hurry and floated down the river Meuse for many days—slowly floated through the flat lands of Holland to Rotterdam, where they found the *John of Yarmouth*, a vessel trading with Hull, whose English flag should give them some protection.

Arrived at Harwich two of the Fathers set off to find Thomas Weld of Lulworth Castle, a former pupil and a wealthy man. He offered them his house at Stonyhurst, it being then unused, with its grandeur tumbling to decay in the wilds of Lancashire.

Thither—for Stonyhurst—set off the little pilgrim-band. What a romantic and beautiful pilgrimage it must have been. It was in the month of August, when the rich harvest of England's eastern counties was in full swing. The fine towers of the churches

THE COURTYARD

rise from the great fields of dazzling gold or shimmering white where the corn is being slowly shorn by the sickles of the reapers. The corn or the stubble stretch for miles almost unbroken by woods, or hills, or towns. By the flat shore the little ship calls at Yarmouth, possibly for bloaters, then to Hull, where our travellers take to a slower barge sailing up the estuary and the Ouse to Selby—fifty-five miles of English river-side scenery in autumn's golden prime in peace.

Leeds was safely reached, but not the great town we know to-day, though Kirkstall's ruined pile would then be there for them to see. A boat on the canal to Skipton helps them on their way, and then comes the tramp across the hills, the backbone of England.

Let us review the wanderers here. There are rather more than twenty, mostly English, some French. The Jesuit Fathers would be in their black habits, the boys in faded uniform of blue coat, red vest, buff breeches, grey stockings, and wonderful caps of leather and fur. The natives call them foreigners—Frenchmen who have killed their King, and are dangerous. They are treading in the footsteps of Oliver and his Ironsides when they hurried in hot haste over these same moorland tracks exactly a hundred and forty-six years before. Cromwell broke for ever the power of King and Pope in England, but here, in his footsteps, is the seed of his enemies, the pioneers of a great army, stealthily, steadily marching on.

The steep and stony ways make their last day's pilgrimage an arduous one. Footsore and weary their boots are wearing out. A high-born Clifford ties on his soles with bits of string. They sit on every doorstep or on stones by the wayside, but unfaltering hope sustains them. "Think not of rest though dreams

STONYHURST HALL

be sweet." The ridge is crossed. The towers of Stonyhurst gleam in the western sky. The Promised Land is in sight. The old home that is to be their future home is won at last. The door is fast locked for the house is empty and desolate, but entrance is made through a window, and the triumphant strains of the Te Deum echo in the empty corridors and ring among the rafters of the ruined hall.

Food and beds are scarce, but fresh air and fatigue are better than feather-beds to make boys sleep. For evening prayers they kneel in a row, dozing, and nodding, till one, tumbling forward, overbalances the lot and down they all go. There were only twelve scholars on that day of entry—the 29th of August 1794.

The school grew rapidly in spite of its poverty, and the old house needed continual repairs, rebuilding or enlargement. The floors were of flags, the walls bare, and the heating by fireplaces only. A precise youth has left the dimensions of the grate in the school-room. Length 1 ft. $1\frac{1}{2}$ in. Depth 0 ft. 8 in. Breadth at top 0 ft. $6\frac{3}{4}$ in. Breadth at bottom 0 ft. $3\frac{5}{8}$ in. Perhaps he was what the natives would call "nesh": for the cold up there in winter would be enough to chill a southerner to the marrow.

A Spartan simplicity seems to have ruled throughout the College. For breakfast and for supper the boys had a bowl of bread and milk, and that is what I have had for the greater part of a life that is lengthening out, though I always had fat bacon to the new milk in the morning.

' For many years the Fathers seem to have clung with an intense conservatism to the foreign customs of the College. The boys never went home for holidays in the early times. Then they had a month in the autumn, but not until recently, did they go home at Christmas. Their cricket was a fossilised survival

THE CRICKET OF BARBARIANS

of the cricket of the England they had left two hundred years before. They played single-wicket with a stone, like a small milestone (on which no one was allowed to sit), for a wicket, and a long club for a

THE YEW WALK

bat. The bowling would be "underhand sneaks," for a full pitch, or even a first hop was not counted as a proper ball to bowl a batsman out, unless he struck at it. The game was on gravel and considered far superior to the ordinary, or "London," cricket of the outer barbarians.

Allowing the boys to go home for holidays, doubtless, started another leak in the hide-bound rules of classical education, for, when at home, they would play "London" cricket, or the cricket of the heretics, and then want to introduce the dreadful innovation at Stonyhurst, but it was not until 1886 that the old-fashioned cricket was given up and a glass showcase bought for the bats and ball.

About the same time the old rules of football gave way to the modern Association game, and that has probably run out other games as it has done elsewhere.

Salmon fishing is a very rare sport for school-boys, but Stonyhurst possesses miles of fishing-rights on its neighbouring rivers. Mention is made of four hundred "morts," or sea-trout being taken in one day on the Hodder, and also salmon, though it is said the latter "taste th' same as th' watter smells" in these populous days.

Having mentioned the sports of the College, I must attempt something about its studies, though my incapacity is greater. In fact, the reading of Father Gerard's book has driven me so often to the Latin dictionary that, in school-boy phrase, "I chuckt it" and am content with the English. Why is it, that with some men Latin vanishes while other lessons remain? I was lately wearily waiting at a railway station, and noticed the hands of the clock were exactly over one another at twelve. Then I wondered when they would be exactly over one another again. The puzzle interested me, and memory brought back the fact that this was a sum in algebra at Cheltenham College fifty years ago. I mentally worked it out, and commend the sum to boys of all ages. Is it use that kept arithmetic alive while the unused Latin died?

With apologies for the digression, I must note

THE REFECTORY

that Latin and languages were the main subjects taught at Stonyhurst, very little notice being taken of mathematics or science; but even here great changes have taken place in recent years. At one time the boys had to talk in Latin; the College became "Collegium Saxosylvanum," nine syllables instead of five; and the small boys who blew up the bladders in the footballs, or football-blowers, became "pilæ pedalis inflatores."

This unnecessary infliction was probably put upon the boys in accordance with the prayer of St. Ignatius, the founder of "the Society of Jesus," for he prayed that his followers might never lack tribulation, and here was tribulation indeed on the buoyant spirits of youth.

As a more modern spirit has come over the College, and its comforts have grown, the number of students has greatly increased, until, of late years, three hundred have been there at once. The absolute ownership of the Hall and the estates of Stonyhurst and Hodder, with one hundred acres of land, was made over to the Society by Mr. Weld on the 31st of July 1809, the anniversary of the Feast of St. Ignatius, and, on the next anniversary, he treated the boys to a dinner and sang them a song which unhappily brought on an apoplectic fit. He had had fifteen children and large estates, and was the founder of the College.

The noblest room is the Refectory, the old hall of the Hall. It must be a great privilege to any boys to have their meals in a place so interesting historically, architecturally, and decked with the trophies of the chase; for among the pictures of saints or holy men are the heads of stags, zebra, moose, and some naughty boys may possibly prefer the animals. Under the Minstrels Gallery is Oliver Cromwell's table, a priceless bit of old furniture. Along the front of the gallery is an ancient inscription in three languages;

OLIVER CROMWELL'S TABLE AND THE MINSTRELS GALLERY

the centre part of it may be read in our photograph, if the reader observe that roses or other conventional ornaments are between some of the words. "Quant je puis × Hugo Sherburn × Armig × me fieri fecit × Ao × Dni × M × ccccc × xxiij × Et sicut fuit voluntas in celo sic fiat." The first three words form the old motto of the Sherburns, and are very proper in their place, though it does seem superfluous for boys at mealtimes to be reminded to eat as much as they can. For the benefit of those who like myself have very little Latin, I venture to give a translation of the latter part: "And as was the Will in heaven so be it done," or, in more familiar words, "Thy will be done in earth as it is in heaven."

For those who are fond of heraldry, there are many emblazoned shields of arms in the windows, and, as would be expected, the treasures of the College in works of art, antiquities, and relics are very great, more than I have space or abilities to chronicle. I did notice the stuffed birds and beasts and the large aviary in the garden. They brought to my remembrance Charles Waterton, whose "Wanderings of a Naturalist" and whose sanctuary on his own estate for all things but the Hanoverian (or now common) rat, were once of the greatest interest to me. In 1796 he became a Stonyhurst boy, whose keen pursuit of natural history earned for him the honorary appointment of rat-catcher to the College. He was a rigid teetotaller, who said he built the high wall round his park at Walton Hall from the money saved by never spending any on intoxicating drink. He never slept in a bed, and lived frugally for eighty-three years.

The greatest treasure in the College, and worthy of special mention, is the manuscript Gospel of St. John that was taken from the tomb of St. Cuthbert in Durham Cathedral in 1104. In 1828 a Dr. Raine wrote an account of the life and many burials of St. Cuthbert, who appears to have been reinterred about ten times. There are two histories of his translation, or, in other words, the violation of his grave in 1104, when the manuscript Gospel that is now at Stonyhurst was taken, though the head of St. Oswald, a golden chalice, and many other relics were left. When the officers of the great King Henry VIII. plundered the shrine they took everything they could sell even to the ring off the dead man's finger, but they missed the golden cross on his breast, for it was hidden in the vestments. That was reserved for the last resurrectionists, the Dean and Chapter of Durham, who, in 1827, took it with other things under the plea of preserving that which the grave had preserved for more than twelve hundred years.

This plundering of the dead in time of peace is done by the clergy. In time of war, when savage heathendom reigns supreme, any one caught plundering the dead is instantly shot.

In 1827 it was found that the outermost coffin over St. Cuthbert's remains was warped and rotting, though it was new in 1542; while the innermost coffin of 698, fully described in 1104, had the carvings in the oak quite plain to be seen—"Johannis," with a book being one of them.

How passing strange it is that this manuscript, with its twelve centuries of history, is now at Stonyhurst, and how infinitely better it must be for boys to be educated in an old English Hall—educated by their environment, not by their lessons only, for lessons may be useless—than for them to be crammed in a modern building destitute of art and history, pent up in noisy street with clanging iron and shrieking steam, while all around them rests an unknown land—the relic strewn land of England.

HARDWICK HALL

"Hardwick Hall
More glass than wall"

stands staring and glaring, flaunting and flaring its comfortless magnificence, far and wide beyond its withered oaks, over the cold bare hills of central Derbyshire—bleak hills that are white and poor with hard lime or black and richer where men delve for dirty coal.

If the sun should struggle through the mists or smoky clouds and shine on Hardwick's glaring glass the stranger from afar would think he saw a glittering mansion in the sky; but in many places the glitter only hides the hard stone wall behind, for the house reflects the cold, hard woman who built it and whose smiles or glittering eye merely lured her victims to their doom.

"Bess of Hardwick" took good care that as long as her stately house of Hardwick lasted all men should know that she had built it, though she might retire with her grandeur to a holier place while she was "expecting a glorious resurrection." High aloft on the parapet, as a sign against the sky, are the letters E. S. for her initials and the coveted crown of the countess. Under our feet in the flower beds of the garden we may stumble over E. S. From the post of honour on the fireplace E. S. glares at us. On chairs and pictures, here, there, and everywhere is E. S., until we, like her worn and wearied husbands, wonder whither we can flee to get beyond her.

Bess of Hardwick was a thorough Derbyshire woman,

but cleverer and far more successful than others can hope to be. She was shrewd, close-fisted, and hard-bitten. She wore out four husbands, and might have had another if the last had not left her to save his life. She cleaned them out of every shilling they possessed, though their children and relatives might starve. She mixed her breed with royalty and had a

HARDWICK HALL

granddaughter who might have been Queen of England. If that had come to pass, how heaven's high portals would have been flung open for her while the archbishop flattered her more than ever, for she was exceeding rich, but now she is merely "expecting a glorious resurrection," and in these days of church restorations things go oft awry.

It is a pity we know nothing of the childhood of "our Bess." Folk-lore teaches us that those who "get their teeth" so early and so often into things in general are born with them. If there had been a recording angel in the old house at Hardwick where Bess was born we might have heard that she was born hard-bitten and close-fisted. Doubtless her forebears, like other Derbyshire folk, had inherited the tightly clenching fingers that are said to be necessary in the struggle for existence on the bare, cold hills and the sterile soil, and she, like they, could live where other folk would starve.

We are told she was "beautiful and discreet" when married at the early age of fourteen, but if she had been as beautiful as the golden-haired angels in the illuminated manuscripts of the time, she could hardly have been discreet enough for the marriage settlements. They provided that all the estates and wealth of the young squire, Barlow of Barlow, who married her, should be settled on her and her heirs. Her father had long been dead, so there must have been a money-grubbing, match-making mamma, with a local lawyer, who would circumvent heaven, somewhere in the background. Somebody soon got rid of the happy bridegroom, though the settled estates were left to cheer the bereaved. Nothing is known as to what was done. Perhaps it happened in the nine months' winter when strangers were scarce and everywhere snowed up, but the great fact remains that Bessy Hardwick became a wealthy young widow, more "beautiful and discreet" than she was before she entered the holy estate of matrimony.

Her next venture was after a title. One dark night, it was two hours after midnight by his own telling, she was wed to a man who had already disposed of two wives, and perhaps fondly imagined he could manage any woman. On his portrait at Hardwick it is plainly written where, or to what, she drove him. They had a family—her only family; but he was soon sent to his account, and the blooming

widow was richer than ever; discreeter with children to rear and provide for; and possibly, as a mother, more beautiful.

She soon found another knight who had lands, and rank, and family. It was the lands she wanted: if they were in Gloucestershire they could be sold and the money could buy many times their acres nearer to Hardwick. She persuaded him to marry her, and to settle all his estates on her and her heirs, leaving his daughters to perish, for she would cherish and comfort him all the days of his life. The bargain was made, and as might be expected, his days were few. His portrait in the long gallery shows that he lost all his hair. Let us hope it came off naturally. He was soon under the sod, and for the third time the widow arose from the abyss of matrimony richer than ever, discreeter with a fuller knowledge of the wicked ways of men, and beautiful still if the hard lines and wrinkles could be kept from too strong a light: and the candles of that day and place were mostly rushlights.

With all these accumulations of wealth, wisdom, and beauty our Derbyshire lady made up her mind to wed the proudest of England's peers—Talbot, Earl of Shrewsbury, a name historical, with broad lands at its back; but the situation was complicated by children. He would not treat his children as her last husband had treated his. He was honourable and high-minded, though said to be "half a Papist." Her Pope was herself. She twisted him round her fingers, married her eldest son to his daughter, the Lady Grace, and her youngest daughter, Mary, to his son and eventual heir, and thus having secured the estates to the family, dragged him to the altar for the better temporal management of them, and the never-fading title of Countess for herself.

All went merry as a marriage-bell—for a time.

"SHE-DEVILS"

Here is an extract from one of his letters to her. "I thank you swete wone for your podengs and venyson." The sauce to them was to follow hereafter, when he got something to his pudding he had never bargained for.

Elizabeth, Queen of England, considering where she could get a cheap and safe prison for her cousin, the

THE OLD HALL AND GATEHOUSE TO HARDWICK HALL

Queen of Scots, fixed upon the coldest and dreariest hills in the centre of England, where the climate would not conduce to longevity, and where rescuers would be lost in the wilderness; and as a guardian or gaoler she confided the royal captive to the Earl of Shrewsbury, who had lately entered into the bonds of matrimony with the Queen of Hardwick.

A moment's pity let us spare for this poor Earl at the terrible troubles that fell upon him from these three women. When he kissed the hand of one for freeing him from the other two, he called them "devils." Each one was utterly unscrupulous in her selfishness, and clever. With a fair start his Countess would have won all the stakes from the other two. She kept her wits about her with wary eyes and ears wide open. The Countess of Lennox, aunt and mother-in-law to the Queen of Scots, accompanied by her son, Charles Stuart, the brother-in-law of the Queen, came to visit her. There must have been some sweet, seducing, "puddings and venison" here, for Charles Stuart, probable heir to the thrones of England and Scotland, was married to Bess of Hardwick junior before the outraged Good Queen Bess of England, with all her spies, jealousies, and suspicions, had heard of the match. Of course she was furious; marriage in young courtiers was the sin she never forgave. She was never married herself, neither was her mother, and she would not allow it in any but common folk. The Countess was imprisoned in the Tower—not for her crimes, but for her management of matters matrimonial.

The Earl could not be imprisoned, for he had to guard the imprisoned Queen, and he laid all the blame on his wife, who was always troubling him to get her daughter married to some nobleman, "to dele forre my Lord Rutland, my Lord Sussex, my Lord Wharton, and sundry others."

Elizabeth would doubtless have imprisoned the newly married couple in separate cells, but she was too late. There was a child on the way; no time had been lost, for the old lady was very careful of all details; and if the child were a wench it would be next heir to the throne after Queen Mary or her son James; and if it were a man-child, it would probably be preferred as an Englishman to the half-daft Scotchman.

What a nice "kettle of fish!" The witch who ruled England had got the other witches in her power,

IN THE GALLERY

but dare not do what she would like to do with them. The suggestion of an accident at Chartley, where there was a deep moat, came in the future. The Earl of Shrewsbury was a most unwilling, but honourable, custodian of the Queen of Scots. His wily Countess from her imprisonment was justified in often asking how they were going on, and doubtless she discreetly made suggestions that made Elizabeth more jealous than ever of Mary, and as the chief danger was in Mary, the two Elizabeths had better be friends and work together for their mutual good.

The Countess being forgiven by the Queen, was free to manage her estates and enjoy herself. The following extracts from a letter to her Lord, explain themselves. "I preye you lette me knowe yf I shall have the tone of iron. You promysed to sende me money afore thys tyme to by oxxen, but I se out of syght out of mynde wt you. I wyll sende you the byll of my wode stoffe . . . yf you wolde comande your wagener to brynge yt to Hardwycke." That is, he must pay her for her wood and cart it—"What's yours is mine, and what's mine's my own." "Here is nether malte nor hoppes. The malte cume last ys so vary yll and stynkenge, none of my workmen wyll drynke it. . . . Come ether afore Medsomer or not thys yere. God send my jewell helthe. E. Shrowesbury. I have sente you letyes: I have nothynge els to send. Lette me here how you, your charge *and love* dothe. It were well you sente fore or fyve peces of the great hangeings that they myghte be put oup, and some carpetes."

The discreetness that Bess of Hardwick displayed in her youth was gradually lost in the rapacity of the avarice that increases with age. Here are extracts from letters of the Earl, wherein he says she calls him knave, fool, and beast to his face. "My wyked and malysyous wyfe is my professed enemy . . . a bad

THE STAIRS

woman who, with her children, speak sclanderouslie of me ... never quyet to satisfie her gredie appetite for money ... and compassed dailie with those that moste maliciously hated me."

There is also the testimony of the Bishop of Lichfield and Coventry, who writes to the Earl that he "thinks her a sharp and bitter shrewe, and therefore lieke enough to shorten y'r life if shee should kepe yow company." This bishop says most women are shrewes, and it reminds me of the one who reproved his wicked page-boy by asking him: "Who is it sees and hears all we do, and in whose sight even I am but a poor worm," and the naughty boy replied: "Please, sir, that's the missus."

The days of sweet puddings and venison were gone, and the Countess cared for nothing but the money she could make from the estates. By stirring up the jealousies and fears of Elizabeth, she got the control of the Earl's property, while he was virtually a prisoner in charge of his prisoner, with £500 a year allowed him just to keep Mary and himself alive.

The wretched man was at last released from the charge of the Queen of Scots, whose end we all know, and his came soon after. His wife again became a blooming widow with all her blushing honours thick upon her. I cannot find any record of her blushing, but here is a bit from a letter written by her daughter, the future Countess of Shrewsbury, to Sir Thomas Stanhope. She says he is "more ugly in shape than the vilest toad in the world ... hopes he may have all the plagues and miseries that may befall such a caitiff, and be damned perpetually in hell-fire."

We are told this lady had the happiness to dispose of her three daughters in marriage to noble Earls—the greatest names in England's history. But what about the poor husbands, and through how many generations did the lady-like manners descend?

THE DISPOSAL OF THE FAMILY

Here is a short account of the lovely and wretched Arabella Stuart, the child that was born of the younger Bess of Hardwick. Her father was soon disposed of,

TAPESTRY
Showing the story of Ulysses

and shortly afterwards her mother "took good ways." Elizabeth would take care there were no more children so near to the throne. Her grandmother, our discreet old lady, took charge of Arabella, and there were soon schemes of marriage, one of them being to her cousin

James. If she had married him, or if he had died childless, she would have been Queen of England. He would not allow her to marry anybody, and a foreigner, free from local jealousies, was married to him. Her grandmother died, and the orphan Arabella was not able to cope with her enemies. She married a young Seymour, an alliance with another great English house that frightened the wretched King James I. into imprisoning her in the Tower for life, driving her into insanity and death, because she might perchance have brought forth better kings than his breed.

This is another bit of the history of our land and people that makes me wonder how we poor English suffered and endured the murderers, robbers, and villains, as Kings, through so many centuries. Reckon them all up—faithfully and charitably—from Henry VIII. to the vilest of the Georges. Oliver was not a King, and Dutch William, with his Mary and her fat sister Anne, were passable. Is there one other who even tried to do right? From such Kings, Good Lord, deliver us! is one of the omissions from our Litany.

The faces that look down on us from the walls of Hardwick, and that haunt us with their sad histories, would be excuse enough for many digressions. Look at the quaint and pretty child named Arabella, nursing its doll. Look also at the despicable James who tortured her to death, and see also in a place of honour "the Virgin Queen" whom the greatest poet thought it better to call "A most unspotted lily." Judge her as she stands, from feet to head, or from head to feet, and say if you can find the lily among the spots, or think to yourself, but don't say, what she does look like.

There is an excellent portrait of the great lady of Hardwick, whose home we have come to see. No doubt it flatters her, or she would not have paid for it, but the artist has contrived to show her shrewd,

"THE MOST UNSPOTTED LILY"

hard features, looking fairly well encircled with a wondrous ruff, and crowned with a Marie Stuart cap. The hands are not the least like the originals; I feel confident of that. They should have bony knuckles,

THE GATEHOUSE

all tightly clenched on something or somebody; but the artists of those days generally left their pupils to fill in hands all alike, with long, tapering fingers, of conventional pattern. I asked X to photograph this picture, but he shuddered and sighed, as he told me I knew nothing of married life. "Let the galled jade

THE PRESENCE CHAMBER

wince." We have heard that ignorance is bliss sometimes, but why should the readers of this book be denied the pleasure of studying the features of the notorious Bess of Hardwick?

We are not giving a full-sized photograph of the house, for there is no beauty in it. It is as regular, angular, and hard-faced as its builder. There is no doubt it was built in the years 1590-97, when the old lady was a widow again, and noblemen with estates were aware of her. Any one with her active habits must be doing something, or she would pine and die, therefore she took refuge in building magnificently. It is a little puzzling to strangers to find what the letters E. S. stand for as her initials. I searched the dictionary of National Biography for her life, under the letter H for Hardwick, but it was not there; then under S, but it was not there; it is given under T.

I also found a copy of her will, whereby she leaves all her "Plate and Furniture to stand entayled" as heirlooms at her house at Hardwick, to continue and remain there. Accompanying the will is an inventory of the furniture and pictures. Here are a few extracts: "Seven pieces of Hangings of Embroidery of Cloathe of Gold and Silver Cloath of Tissue, Velvet of sundry colours, and Needle-work twelve foot deep. Six curtains of Blew and Satten stripte with gold and silver, and laised with Gold Lace. A purple Sarsenett Quilt. A great chair, joyned Stools. A little desk of Mother of Pearl."

It would be a pity to omit the bequest to Arabella. " . . . to Arabella Stewart my Christal Glass framed with Silver and guilt" (*sic*, what a mistake!) "and set with Lapis Lazarus and Agget . . . all my Pearl and Jewels and . . . £1000 in money. . . . To the Queen £200 for a Cupp of Gold, praying her to accept that poor Widow's Mite, and be good and gracious to her poor Grandchild, Arabella Stewart, a

THE GALLERY

desolate Orphan." Unfortunately there comes a codicil at the end revoking all the gifts to Arabella. Would the revocation include the "Cupp" that was to bribe the Queen? We might trust the unspotted Lily for that if it had not pleased the Lord to take her first.

Bess of Hardwick appears to have been more accommodating in her religious views than she was in money matters. Her second husband, Sir William Cavendish, was what was politely termed "a visitor" of the robbed abbeys. At Lilleshall alone, he is said to have bought thirty-four embroidered copes for £3. Some of them, or parts of them, are in the chapel at Hardwick now. Becoming rich on the spoils of the religious houses, he and his lady went back to Romanism when Mary came to the throne, for Queen Mary and Gardiner, Bishop of Winchester, were sponsors for Charles Cavendish, the third son. Then, when Elizabeth was Queen, our heroine 'verted again. After that, who can say she was self-opinionated?

These bits of the histories of the great ones of the earth may be interesting to the common folk, whose duty it is to order themselves lowly and reverently to all their betters, but there are more than two hundred portraits at Hardwick, from kings and queens as plenty as blackberries down to the Rev. Mr. Smith and "a lady of unblemished character." This book could not contain all the good things about them.

In addition to this great collection of oil-paintings of historical personages, there is at Hardwick more old tapestry than we have seen in all the houses we have ever been in. Some of it is doubtless that mentioned in the letter of the Countess on page 362, and also in her will. The walls of the great gallery, 166 feet in length and 26 feet in height, are hung with tapestry behind the pictures. Each window in this room is said to contain 1500 panes of glass. The presence chamber shown on page 361, is hung round

MORTLAKE TAPESTRY

with Brussels tapestry by Andreas Van Dries illustrating the history of Ulysses. The Royal Arms over the mantelpiece show the dragon of Wales as a supporter, it being used by the Tudors and older than the unicorn.

The photograph shown on the preceding page was not taken for the tapestry, but for the "nonsuch" chest below it, as we had had some discussion about similar chests. There is another at Arundel. I think the chest has the initials G. T. for Gilbert Talbot, the seventh Earl of Shrewsbury. When the photograph was printed, it was a surprise to see that even the threads in the tapestry had shown themselves, and we wished we had taken more tapestry where it was in a good light. As a rule it is dangerous to photograph rooms where there are pictures, especially those with glass fronts, as the light reflects and spoils the photograph; but in this case the tapestry "came out" beautifully.

The corner of the dining-room, with its oaken panelling, old portraits, and furniture, makes a very fine picture. We may here read, mark, learn, and inwardly digest "the conclvsion of all thinges is to feare God and keepe his commavndementes": it being checked, initialled, and dated by E. S. 1597, she being then in her eightieth year, and having been scratting and scraping the money together "by hook or by crook" for sixty years. She certainly had great experience and she may have heard that in some countries "honesty is said to be the best policy."

There is another room to be specially mentioned, and that is the one called after Mary Queen of Scots. There can be no doubt that she was never in this house, for it was not built until after her death. The Fotheringay tragedy was done in 1587, and this room bears the date 1599, with the Arms of Scotland, the initials M. R., and Marie Stewart par la grace de Dieu Royne d'Ecosse, Douairière de France. The

THE DINING-ROOM

THE NEEDLEWORK OF THE QUEEN OF SCOTS

THE DRAWING-ROOM

needlework, the bed curtains, and the quilt were the work of the captive Queen and her maidens, and were doubtless brought to Hardwick from Sheffield or Tutbury, or wherever they were wrought.

I feel utterly incompetent to describe the furniture, fittings, and pictures that are in Hardwick Hall. If I could do it, the description would be too long for this book, therefore the reader may know that about one per cent. of the contents is all I have room to mention. One great fact must be recorded, and that is the exceedingly good taste with which everything is preserved. There are no attempts to "restore," improve, age, or alter anything. The frayed threads of silk may hang from embroidered needlework or even from the seats of chairs, or from ancient vestments. It is better to let them hang in natural and inevitable decay than to let some furniture restorer meddle with them. The Duke wishes them to be preserved, not altered, and fortunately he has the courage of his opinions and his knowledge.

I cannot even give the names of all the rooms we photographed, for we were turned loose and left alone for hours; that being very delightful at the time, but rather bothering afterwards. For instance, the preceding page, I think, shows the drawing-room. There is a wonderful mantelpiece, with stags supporting the arms of the great Countess, and a jumble of Latin words about stags and their blood, horns, eyes, and feet, to assert that noble as the stag is, it is nobler by serving the Countess; and therefore one might irreverently add, it would be noblest of all when she ate it.

The small pictures on the panelling of this room as shown in the photograph and beginning on the left are, I believe: 1st, Arabella Stewart with her doll; 4th, Henry VIII.; 5th, Edward VI.; 6th, Henry VII.; Katharine of Aragon and some doubtful ones. I took the liberty of pulling the cover off one of the

THE FIREPLACE IN THE HALL

chairs that it might be photographed, but, unfortunately, the chair is in a corner of the picture.

There is an historical chair that must be noted, for it came from the Cock and Pynot Inn on Whittington Moor, near Chesterfield, and was used by the first Duke of Devonshire when he met Lord Danby to take counsel about inviting William of Orange to be King of England. It is shown on the preceding page, with its back towards the fireplace in the hall, having been turned by me that it might be in a better light.

Other photographs of the hall must tell their own tale. The old, oak table is there, thirty feet in length. Another table is dated 1697, H. N., and there is a pair of boots that bring to mind the old lines—

> "He who would these boots displace
> Must meet Bombastes face to face."

The quantities of old arms and armour, miles of fine tapestry, furniture without end, both old and good—there being several of the couches that used to be placed at the foot of the big bedsteads—relics and curiosities of all kinds must be passed over or we shall never have done. We must say good-bye to Bess of Hardwick and all her widow's mites and jewels framed in "guilt," for this day we have been heirs to her wealth, and enjoyed her grandeur quite as much as she herself ever did. She enjoyed herself in two ways—match-making and building. Perhaps she liked a bit of scolding also, but that would only be natural. When she became too old to make love-matches, the pleasure of building was all that she had left, and she must go on planning, scheming, building while life lasted. It needed no witch to tell her that. She was witch enough herself to know it and to feel it. What a terrible tough old woman she must have been to endure the nine months' Arctic winters of Derbyshire hills in a place like Hardwick.

ENTRANCE TO THE HALL

The frosts there split the rocks, and the skinny sheep are starved to death when the east wind smothers all things with the deeply drifted snow, while the hardy natives cower behind their stone walls, saving their funeral expenses as long as ever they can.

"Our Bess" struggled on to her ninetieth winter, an exceptionally severe winter, when all building stopped and everything froze even to the marrow of her bones. There was nothing to do and nought to live for, but she held fast to dear life till the worst of the cold had well nigh gone, for the half of February had past, then her strong will was worn down, and the firm lips relaxed in death.

I am afraid we did not trouble ourselves much about Bess, or mourn for her while we were at Hardwick. We were too busy and happy. The few and fleeting hours of an October day were crowded with work and energy. There were more pictures to take than X could take, though he never knowingly takes an ugly one.

The chief constable of the county took us into custody after we had been loitering with intent in a most suspicious manner. He treated us very well, for we all three sat on the steps to the front door, and had an excellent lunch to prepare us for the long ride in his motor-car. As we whizzed through the park it amused me greatly to notice the deer. This devil's whirlwind was new to them. Their best pace was nothing to it, and many crouched as flat as they could squeeze themselves on the ground, with their heads and necks stretched out flat though they could not hide their horns. They lay motionless as long as I could see them.

As we rushed along the country lanes, we saw some straggling sheep before us that a farmer was apparently trying to separate, but, losing his temper, he picked up his dog by its neck and held it up while

THE HALL

he savagely kicked its hind quarters. "Stop that" was shouted at him as the car pulled up alongside. "Who the hell are you. Mind your own business," was the reply. "I am the chief constable of the county. This is my business, and I ask your name and address." The man's face turned in colour from a dirty purple to a dirty yellow. He took his hat off and kept it off, for he had evidently been reared in a ducal atmosphere, perhaps in a ducal charity school. He said he "was only learning the brute manners; dogs were senseless things and had to be learnt manners." Still, the name and address were wanted, that a lesson might be given in the teaching of manners to brutes, even in that country.

Here is a small extract from a letter of the Earl of Shrewsbury that I made when reading old documents about Hardwick. It is to the Justices of the Peace for Derbyshire: " . . . as for the smaleness of beastes yt are bredde in Derbyshire, every oxe should be v foote and eyghte inches in lengethe; so as if ther be not of yt sise in or owne contrey, we muste cause them to be boughte in Lancashyre or els wher." That was written more than three hundred years ago, and the poor, clemmed ricklings are little better now; but it is not their fault for they cannot help it.

We were driven round by Bolsover's stately, ruined castle, but had little time to see it for the light was fading, and many steep and grimy hills lay between us and Chesterfield. Our custodian's Humber car took the hills in a frolic, as it seemed to swallow them. The famous crooked spire of Chesterfield soon came in sight, looking as if the devil had tried to twist its neck and left it toppling over ready to fall on the church below. We caught a train for Sheffield to take us home, X being very dissatisfied with its pace. Even when we had changed into another and rushed down the long decline from Derbyshire to

Cheshire, he said "it was beastly slow after the motor-car," though all trains go down that bank at seventy miles an hour or thereabouts.

Worse was to come, for we finished the day's journey in a hansom cab with a poor old "tit" that hobbled and shuffled, tumbling from one shaft to another, as every minute its head was nearly jerked off from above, and we with the precious glass plates of the photographs were tossed in all ways.

A FIREPLACE AT HARDWICK

NORMAN HALL

ON one of Cheshire's pleasant hills there is a timeworn house with a grand name but no history—not a scrap of history, legend, or tale that I can learn, and yet its name with its beautiful country should bring wealth for a magnificent restoration, if it were only known to some of our neighbours on whom new riches have rolled.

NORMAN HALL

Norman Hall—what an attraction to an enterprising member of the great families of Smith, or Jones, or Brown, or Robinson, who can read and write and has made tons of money (it not being necessary that he should speak English), and who sighs for the old house at home where his forefathers dwelt. He finds it here, dismantled, derelict and desolate, but ready to revive under his genius and his gold. More than once has plain Mr. Smith as-

NORMAN HALL

sumed a Norman name and appropriated ancestors as much akin to him as was Mr. Tubal-Cain who was fond of brass on the east side of the garden of Eden. He has even got barristers, "gentlemen learned in the law," who ought to have been above selling themselves, to edit and endorse his fudge. Here might be the long-lost home of a romantic race!

NORMAN HALL

For ages, Cheshire's knights and esquires with their serfs and vassals served under their Earls, the Kings of England, in their wars beyond the sea—singing with the troubadours "Our King is gone to Normandy;" and some battered, war-worn warrior, whose luck had brought him home again, may have built this "Norman Hall" on the land where he was born. Now he is "gone hence." There is no record of his life or death. There is no legend or tale. The heirs and the mourners are gone. The sighs have ceased. The very name and memory are all forgotten.

MY FATHER'S DOGS
From an oil-painting by CALVERT

THE GUARDIANS OF THE HOME

AS three dogs—sire, son, and grandson—have been the watchful guardians of my home for forty years, they deserve some better memorial than the scattered notices that I have hitherto given them.

It was well known that this old Parsonage house was haunted when we came to live here; in fact it was said the ghosts had partly scared the parsons away, but I thought some of those ghosts might be rats, and my father's dogs being setters, were above rats, therefore I welcomed a rough bristle-haired rat-catching terrier that followed me home one day, and called him Japhet as he seemed to be in search of his father. He was such a dear, little, cock-tailed pup, looked so happy, and had such a keen enjoyment of his life, especially when he could get his teeth into anything that had fur on it, that he became quite a treasure, and, fortunately, I made a sketch of him in his favourite attitude looking out of the window. One day there was a boy came up the drive whose behaviour displeased him, so he jumped crash through the glass, and before the bad boy could say "Knife," he was nabbed.

Like most dogs and men he went worse tempered as he grew older, and at last he fought with a young bull-terrier in the night, and was found dead in the morning with his foe nearly dead also, so we buried them in one grave, and their tombstone records—

"They were lovely and pleasant in their lives,
And in their death they were not divided."

That was in March 1875, we having had him about ten years. He was an old English, mongrel terrier of a brown colour and a bit undershot, the better to pin the rats against a wall. A longer-haired Scotch terrier that was also a good ratter at the neighbouring hostel had some pups by him, and I was glad to secure one, the one with the biggest head, to call him Gomer the son of Japhet, and to have him in his father's stead.

Gomer grew up a wonderful dog, with more sense than a deal of folk. He knew when it was Sunday morning, and if the ringers were late with the church bells, he would howl at the proper time whether they rang or not. He could tell whether it was ghosts or rats that made the uncanny noises that so often disturbed us at nights. He would never flinch from anything; but if the intruder was something supernatural, his bristles stood stiffly erect, his eyes followed the invisible, and his growl was deep. If cats or rats were on the rampage he would be as pleased as Punch, and beg of us to have a good hunt. One night he climbed several feet up a holly tree after

a rat that I shot, and weighed to be one pound and a quarter.

When he was full of years and honour, I bought a pure-bred Dandie Dinmont named Gyp (but we called her Meg) to be his mate, and was only just in time to preserve the breed, for he died the next year, and we buried him alongside his father, his gravestone giving the dates of his birth and death, 1874–1889, and stating "There never was a dog like Gomer."

GYP

The pup I had kept for myself had in his younger days several names, Tosspot being one of them, and for many years I was too much occupied with weightier matters to spend as much time with the live stock as I had done. He was not allowed in the house for fear of my Mother falling over him, but no better tenter or wiser dog ever lived. The years of warfare had greatly lessened the cats and rats that had so long troubled us; even the ghosts had mostly ceased, whether they were "laid" or the time of their expiation had ended I don't know (there are more particulars in my "Folk-Lore"); but so many things had happened I had never noticed how old my second Gomer was growing, until by chance I saw his father's

GOMER II

gravestone when playing with him one Sunday afternoon, and found he had long past the allotted age of dogs. A diligent search in old almanacs found the memorandum of his birth on the 12th of August 1888, and he died on the hottest day I ever knew, the thermometer being ninety in the shade, on the first of September 1906.

We buried him the next morning with his fathers by the weeping ash on the lawn where the crocuses flower in the spring, and as I patted him in his grave for the last time, for "no useless coffin enclosed him" and he had died with his tail up as he had lived, I thought of the many legends there were not only in Didsbury but all around, when in similar burning weather the plague had come in the olden times, and the village folk had been buried hurriedly by any one.

For forty years these three dogs would have given their life and all for me. This is all I can give in remembrance of them—

"The rich man's guardian and the poor man's friend
The only creature faithful to the end."

"THERE'S LIFE IN THE OLD DOG YET"
A good tailpiece.

HALE BARNS

ONE of the old homes where my forefathers dwelt, is here shown to those who do not scorn the dwellings of the humble. He who lived in it a hundred years ago, and who probably built it, was a Quaker. The first record that I can find of him is the register of his wedding at Wilmslow on the 8th of January 1771. "James Barratt to Betty Roylance." He had lived on the lonesome, desolate morass known as Lindow Moss, where there had long been a meeting-house of the Friends, and he was one of them, though "barat" is an old word for strife, and a "barrator" is one who is fond of going to law. Two or three miles away from the moss, is the hamlet known as Hale Barns, where there was another lonely old chapel, and near to it James Barratt had his little house, where his grand-daughter kept him company at times, and eighty years afterwards would tell us, her children, the tale of her fright with a snake in his garden.

For a hundred years the house has altered very little. The windows appear to be new and the roof, but all around the modern jerry villa is compassing it about, and the ivy-covered chapel is peart with a lych gate and a belfry—unnecessary superfluities that would have shocked the quiet Quakers.

James Barratt had a daughter named Mary who was betrothed to a Joseph. Joseph and Mary asked for an hour's absence from work, met at Manchester's old church and quietly were wed. Joseph Fletcher was an evangelical Churchman, with a strong distrust or detestation of all papists, Chartists, Irish or foreigners. The wife obeyed the husband, but the grey mare was the better horse, and although she conformed to the Church as by law established she did not desert the ways of the Friends, for her youngest daughter, whose name is spelt Kathrine in the family Bible, had all the careful, methodical management of her affairs and of the

NEAR HALE BARNS

ways of her household that distinguishes the Quakers, and from her I have inherited any good business habits there may be in me.

Joseph Fletcher carried on the trade of a corn and provision dealer at New Cross, Manchester. An old book of his shows entries of flour sold at one hundred and eighteen shillings per load of two hundred and forty pounds; sixpence a pound for brown flour. That famine price was in 1812, the year of Bonaparte's retreat from Moscow, when Europe was in its lowest

MY GREAT-GRANDFATHER'S HOME

depths of woe. In 1819, Peterloo struck terror through Manchester, especially in the shops of the corn trade, where barley meal was the principal food of the poor, the great invention of potatoes being almost unknown.

Through those dark years of the nineteenth century, Joseph and Mary reared their children in a godly, righteous, and sober life. Every Sunday, twice a day, the family marched to church, two and two, like the animals going in the ark; four couples of children and I know not how many of apprentices and servants. Each couple carried a big prayer-book, bound in rough, brown leather, with the name of J. Fletcher on the outside, and wonderful pictures within of the Solemnization of Matrimony and the Publick Baptism of Infants, showing the strange costumes of the eighteenth century, for the books are dated 1795 and have scarce been opened for a hundred years. Why should we pray for those who are past praying for? The poor, soft King: "what mortal ever heard any good of George the Third?" Queen Charlotte, and the Prince with the false curls above the face of vanity. David and his harp may well be shown in agony, for the Evangelicals of the day would not leave his psalms alone:

> "The man is blest that hath not lent
> To wicked men his ear;
> Nor led his life as sinners do,
> Nor sat in scorner's chair."

All those of whom I write are long since dead and buried, and well-nigh forgotten; and though I cannot call any of them back to life, I can show some resemblance of them, and here reproduce the portraits of three. The old Quaker who often fondly told them "civility is cheap and pleases all"; and two of his grand-daughters, Hannah and Kathrine (or Catherine), whose love for one another never faltered. The pictures of the sisters were painted seventy years ago by Benjamin Faulkner; and Hannah Fletcher with her dark auburn hair and rosy cheeks and blue eyes, would be bad to beat to-day.

Though I write thus well of my maternal forbears, it was not from them came the capabilities to write this

HANNAH FLETCHER

book. It was my father's kindred who told me the folk-lore and the legends of the countryside; that gave me the athletic body, the love of sport, the love of an old home, mingled at times with the wandering nomad's life. From earliest times my father's folk had lived on their cattle and on the produce of the land, in isolated farms where the thoughts and customs were of generations and of religions that are almost forgotten. They professed to believe in "Church and State," but, unknown to themselves, there was a far stronger belief in the old pagan customs. The great festivals were Harvest-Home, The Wakes, and Mayday on the twelfth of May, when the cows slept out. At the brewing of the ale the leaven was crossed, as it was in the baking of bread, though my aunts were cross enough when I told them they were like Roman Catholics. The fields of wheat were blazed or fired on old-Christmas eve to scare the witches and the smut from off the corn. The new-born babe's first taste was of rue tea—Rue, "the herb of grace," the bitterest of herbs. The first pancake on Shrove Tuesday was given to the game-fowls. The premature calf was hung in chains above the shippon door that the cows might look upon it and the plague be stayed. When I likened this to the raising of the brazen serpent by Moses in the wilderness, the retort might well come: "Much learning doth make thee mad."

My mother called her first daughter Hannah, after her favourite sister. She was warned that no Anne or Hannah Moss had ever been reared; the name in the family was of the direst omen. Her good common-sense scorned the nonsense. But the child died; the only one of her children that has not lived to old age. It was a sore remembrance with her for more than sixty years. The blazing of the wheat at Standon was stopped, for the custom was too palpably heathenish. In a few years they had to buy their corn from Egypt or their flour from America. The growth of wheat in the parish ceased.

If I as a child hurt myself, my father would tell me to spit upon the place where it was sore, or to rub it, or it might be the cure would be to "touch timber," or to say "Devil, I defy thee" and spit on

IN THE DRAWING-ROOM. THE OLD PARSONAGE

the ground. My mother would tell me "never heed it, nature cures itself, and prevention is better than cure." Fortunately, neither of them had faith in doctors and drugs, and as I sink into "the vale of years" and the spirits of youth fade away, the calm sense of the Friends appeals more strongly to me than ever, for they manage to be fairly happy without the encumbrances of parsons, and with little need for doctors, lawyers, soldiers, and butchers. After mixing with all sorts and conditions of men in jarring religions, politics, trades and sport for fifty years, I think, if my time had to come over again and I had my choice, I would prefer to be a Quaker.

MY QUAKER GREAT-GRANDFATHER

Index

ABBEYFIELD, 38
Aberbran, 119
Aberconwy, 192-194
Aberdovey, 266
Abergavenny, 111
Adeliza, 275
Ale, 34, 48, 294, 296, 306, 314
Arabella Stuart, 357-370
Arms, coats of, 290
Arundel Castle, 267-300
Audley, 56-70
Audley, Sir James, 45-65

BARDS, the, 206, 242, 248
Barmouth, 234, 252
Barratt, James, 385-392
Barthomley, 41-43, 58-71
Bearstone, 93, 95
Beavers, 158
Bess of Hardwick, 346-374
Betley, 60-64
Bettws y Coed, 196, 222
Bishop's palace, 156-161
Bitterns, 162-164
Blaenau Festiniog, 228
Bloody Footmark House, 19-28
Blore Heath, 90, 97
Boar's Head, the, 86
Bolsover, 376
Brecon, 114-118
Broughton, 82, 98-108
Buerton Hall, 109
Bull swimming river, 232

CALDY Isle, 128, 139
Calveley, Sir Hugh, 66, 68, 84
Cardinal Beaufort, 310, 312, 319
Carew, 136
Carmarthen, 127, 142, 174
Carrington, Earl, 197, 210
Castle Martin cattle, 128
Cattle, wild white, 134
Cerrig Cennen Castle, 125
Charity Commissioners, 310-320
Charles I., 216, 288
Chesterfield, 376
Chichester, 301
Church atmosphere, 90, 97, 318
Civil War, the, 41, 82, 100, 132, 192
Cnut, 304
Cockpit in house, 38
Constables, chief, 116, 374
Conwy, 176-204, 236, 238
Cors y Gedol, 244-252
Cotton-spinning, 11-14
Cox, David, 222
Crewe, 58, 80
Crewe, Earl of, 66
Cricket, 339
Crickhowell, 112
Crompton, Sam, 6-18
Cromwell, Oliver, 132, 264, 326, 328, 336, 342
Crosses, 29, 32, 136
Curlews, 226
Customs, old, 390
Cymmer Abbey, 249-254

INDEX

D'Albinis, the, 268, 276
David, St., 148–151, 166
Delves, Sir John, 58–65, 78–86
Derbyshire, 161, 348
Didsbury, 26, 40, 44, 260, 261, 310, 382, 391
Doddington, 45–87
Dog-gate, 35
Dogs, our, 380–384
Dolaugwyn, 262–265
Dolgelly, 232, 266
Dolwyddelan, 202, 216, 226–231
Dorrington, 92
Dovey, the, 266
Dower House, Delves, 84, 87
Dryslwyn Castle, 126
Dukes of Norfolk, 280–292
Dutton, Sir Robert, 58, 59
Dwryd, the, 237
Dysynni, the, 262

Edward I., 151, 188, 228, 238, 243
Effigies of squires, 65–67
Egertons, the, 72–77, 208
Elizabeth, Queen, 184, 221, 284–332, 352, 358
Evans, 264

Fecundity, Welsh, 198, 204
Festiniog, 230, 235
Fitzalans, the, 268, 278
Fletchers, the, 385–392
Flodden, 48, 58, 282
Folk-lore, 390
Fowleshurst, Sir R., 58–68

Gam Davy, 118
Gavelkind, 205
Giraldus, 117, 128, 150, 158, 160

Glyndwr, 118, 238, 249
Greenwich time, 146
Griffith, 64, 186, 200, 264
Gwydyr, 196–221
Gwynn, 264

Hale Barns, 385–392
Hall i' th' Wood, 1–18
Hardwick, 346–377
Harlech, 234–243
Haverfordwest, 138, 142, 174
Hawkstone, Sir John, 58, 72
Heaton Hall, 74–77
Heley Castle, 78–81
Hengwrt, 254–261
Henry VIII., 48, 284, 286, 317, 345, 370
Hiding-hole, 106, 184, 220, 256, 331
Hodder, the, 322, 340, 342
Holbein, 282, 286
Holland, E., heiress, 74
Home of Noble Poverty, 301–321
Honey sop, 314
Hospital of Holy Cross, 305–321
House of Bloody Footmark, 19–28
Howards, the, 268, 280–296
Howell, 194, 200, 249

Jackdaws, 156, 158, 240
James I., 358
Jesuits, the, 322, 332–344
Jones, Inigo, 194, 212, 244

Katharine of Aragon, 292, 370
Kneller, 75

Lamphey Palace, 134
Learning manners, 376

INDEX

Lever Brothers, 2, 4
Llandilo, 126, 142, 174
Llandovery, 121-124
Llanegryn, 260-263
Llanrwst, 194-201
Llanspyddyd, 120-123
Lledr, the, 226
Llewelyn, 176, 194, 198, 227, 252
Loggerheads, the, 102

MAENTWROG, 232, 235
Maison Dieu, 296
Manorbere, 128, 135
"March of the Men of Harlech," 240-243
Marsh the Martyr, 19-23
Mary Queen of Scots, 216, 284, 351-370
Massacre of Barthomley, 41
Mawddach, the, 232, 252
Menevia, 138, 150, 160
Milford Haven, 136-138
Miracle, a, 150
Missionary, duties of a, 160
Mitton, 322
Moel Siabod, 228
Montalt, 278
Montgomery, 266-268
Moss, John, 40
Mucklestone, 90-100

NANNEY, 258, 264
Nesta, 111, 116, 130, 278
Newgale, 144, 170
Noble Poverty, 301-321
Norman Hall, 378

OLD furniture, 14-16, 75, 180, 210-220, 258, 292, 326, 366, 370-372

Oliver Cromwell, 132, 264, 326-328, 336, 342
Otters in Wales, 166
Owen, 130
Owen of Heullys, 161

PARSON, a tame, 208
Pembroke, 128-134, 172
Pennant, 176. 186, 242
Peregrines, 160, 209
Pilgrim's Way, the, 144, 167-174
Plas Mawr, 178-186
Plunder of the poor, 316-319
Poictiers, 45-56
Poorsfield, Didsbury, 310
Poyer shot, 132
Pritchard, Rees, 121

QUAKERS, 385-392

RAMSAY Isle, 144, 160
Richard III., 118, 280, 282
Roast hare, 94
Roch Castle, 172-174
Roses, York and Lancaster, 100
Royal Oak, the 222
Rupert, Prince, 82, 192, 216

ST. Bride's bay, 144, 170
St. Cuthbert's Gospel, 344
St. Davids, 138-175
Salmon, 158, 340
Sandbach, 29-44
School of Technology, Manchester, 11
Shakspere, 282, 292, 312
Sherburne or Shireburn, 308, 324-332
Shrewsbury, Earl of, 350

Siddons, Mrs., 118
Skipton, 328, 336
Skomar, 144
Smithills Hall, 19-28
Snowdon, 193, 228, 234
Solva, 146, 172
Squires, the four, 45-78
Standon, 59, 390
Starkies, the, 4, 9, 14
Starlings, 238-240
Stonyhurst, 322-345
Stuart, Charles, 352
Sunset at St. Davids, 146
Sweat, a holy, 260

Tapestry, 212, 294, 362, 364
Tenby, 128, 136-139
Tewksbury, 77, 152
Thirty-nine Articles, the, 152
Tilting-ground, 274
Towy, the, 124, 127, 141
Towyn, 260, 262
Trecastle, 121
Trefriw, 236
Tretower, 113, 118
Trout, 163

Usk, the, 114-120

Van Dyck, 288
Vanner, 252
Vaughans, the, 118, 244-258

Wakes, 324, 390
Wardley Hall, 19
Waterton, Charles, 344
Welds, the, 332, 334, 342
Wells, the, 142, 174
"Welshman's Candle," 124
Welsh patriots, 248
White Lion, the, 68-71
Wildfowl, 162
Williams, Archbishop, 192
Wilton, Earls of, 74, 76
Winchester, 302-321
Woodcocks, 162, 164
Woolf, 38, 40, 64
Woore, 86
Worcester fight, 41
World's End, the, 130, 184, 274
Wrinehill, 58, 72-76
Wybunbury, 79, 83-87
Wynnes, the, 180-221

THE END

Contents of Preceding Books on Pilgrimages

FIRST BOOK

PILGRIMAGES IN CHESHIRE AND SHROPSHIRE

Dutton Hall—Bunbury Church—Beeston Castle—Utkynton Hall—Farndon—Holt—Malpas—The Old Home of the Egertons—Vale Royal—Tabley old Hall—Gawsworth—Marton Hall—Speke Hall—Battlefield (Shrewsbury)—Haughmond Abbey—Hodnet—Baguley Hall—Hawthorne Hall—Chorley Hall—Soss Moss Hall—Higher Peover—The Royal Oak—Tong—Whiteladies—Woolf's Barn (where the King hid)—Madeley-on-Severn—Atcham—Uriconium—Wroxeter—Buildwas Abbey—The Birthplace of the Prophet—Erbistock—Peels—Cheadle to Prestbury—Woodford Hall—Adlington Hall—Much Wenlock—Easthope—Acton Burnell—Ludlow—Stokesay—Bridgnorth—Dunvall—Shropshire—The best of Cheshire—Church Preen—Church Stretton—Frodesley Lodge—Clun—Diddlebury—Munslow—Millichope—Madeley in Staffordshire—On Pilgrims.

SECOND BOOK

PILGRIMAGES TO OLD HOMES MOSTLY ON THE WELSH BORDER

Alderley—Audlem—Moss Hall—Mucklestone Wood—Ashley—Mees Hall—Ranton Abbey—Swynnerton—Hartington—Tissington—Whittington (the birthplace of Dick)—Jack Mytton's Halston—The end of the World and the Vale of the Cross—Albright Hussey—Preston Gubbals—Myddle—Moreton Corbet—The Home of the Herefords—Ludlow—Leinthall (where the Chicago bull was born)—Weobley (the most beautiful village in England)—The Ley—Clifford Castle on the Wye—Rhyd Spence—Dorstone—Abbey Dore—Kilpeck—Ledbury—Much Marcle—Preston Court—Hereford—Ludlow—Ludford—Orleton Court—Lemster—Eardisland—Bosbury—Dormington Court—Alltyrynys—Llanthony Abbey—Grosmont—Garway—Tintern Abbey—Monmouth—Goodrich Castle—Siddington—Astbury—Little Moreton Hall—Dieulacres Abbey—Leek—Saltersley—Montgomery Castle—Marrington Hall—Lymore, Chirbury

CONTENTS OF PRECEDING BOOKS

—Powysland—Rhyd-y-carw—Talgarth—Park—Macsmawr—Penarth—Penrhos Hall—Trederwen—Trewern Hall—Warburton Old Church—Arley Hall—Minsterley Hall—Caus Castle—Marche Manor—Home of Old Parr of the Pills—Pitchford Hall—Treago Castle—Wythall Court—Manchester's Oldest Home—The Brereton Arms Inn—Shipton Hall, Shropshire—Norbury, Derbyshire—Carden Hall, Cheshire—Barlow Hall, Lancashire—Abney Hall.

THIRD BOOK
PILGRIMAGES TO OLD HOMES

Wells—Glastonbury—Walford Hall—Chartley and the Wild Cattle—Somerford Park—Tutbury—Croxden Abbey—The Standish Pew, Chorley—Houghton Tower—Wrexham—Yale—Bala—Vyrnwy—Haddon Hall—Bradford-on-Avon—Norton St. Philip—Muchelney—Athelney—Taunton—Crowcombe—Cleeve—Dunster—Exmoor Staghunting—Dulverton—Bath—Lytes Cary—Nunney Castle—South Wraxall—Great Chalfield—Stoke-sub-Hamdon—Barrington Court—Bur—Dunster Castle—Compton Wynyates—Baddesley Clinton—Wardley Hall (the House of the Skull)—Worcester—Tewkesbury—Birts-Morton—Huddington Court (the last home of the Gunpowder Plot)—Cleeve Prior—Evesham—Harvington Court—Handforth Hall—Park Hall, Oswestry—Slade Hall—The Riddings—Cockfighting—The Old Parsonage, Didsbury.

WORKS PREVIOUS TO THE ABOVE

A HISTORY OF DIDSBURY
CHRONICLES OF CHEADLE AND GATLEY
FOLK-LORE, OLD CUSTOMS AND TALES OF MY NEIGHBOURS—

Containing the folk-lore and customs relating to births, weddings, burials, festivals, ghosts, lawyers, doctors, parsons, schoolmasters, churchwardens, voters, &c.; a meeting of the Local Board and pilgrimages to the Royal Oak, Boscobel—Hawarden—Blore Heath—Beeston Castle—Peckforton Castle—Barthomley.

A few copies of "Didsbury," price six shillings net.; of "Folk-Lore," half-a-guinea; and of the third "Pilgrimages," a guinea, may be bought from the author and publisher, FLETCHER MOSS, DIDSBURY